THE SOUL GRIND

Fighting for Light Amidst The Trenches

JAYDEE GRAHAM

Launch Pad Publishing

"Jaydee has a natural gift of both empowering and nurturing your soul. *The Soul Grind* is an expression of real, raw authenticity that will inspire you to live and speak your own truth."

-Helene Trager-Kusman, Wellness Blogger, Yoga Teacher and Reiki Healer

"Jaydee Graham has a way of speaking to your soul in a way that helps you heal those parts of you that you may have not even realized needed healing."

-April Murphy, Ph.D, CSW

"Jaydee Graham is like an archaeologist examining her own life in *The Soul Grind*, digging for clues to a truth that applies to more than her own history. The specifics are about her, her family and her struggle to find her truest, best self, but bigger lessons resonate for anyone who has fought to be seen, fought to be heard, fought to be free, fought to be. Her own discoveries hold value for all of us."

-Pam Platt, Writer and Editor

"Jaydee Graham is one of the most resilient souls that I have ever come across and *The Soul Grind* sheds light on that resilience. *The Soul Grind* will not only give you a glimpse into her inspirational self on a very real level, but encourage you to do some soul searching of your own. I truly admire Jaydee's strength in sharing her personal story with the world, because we can all benefit from her voice."

-Casey Sikora, Portfolio Manager

"If you are ready to go on a heartfelt, brave, soul-searching journey, *The Soul Grind* will inspire you to embrace the beautifully vulnerable adventure. Jaydee's story comes to life through her writing, allowing us - her readers - to feel as though we are all on the journey right along with her. Her example will undoubtedly inspire others who are ready to take up space in their own lives by facing pain, reaching out for and accepting support, and rising up from what can feel like and be literal trenches in our lives."

-Dr. Norah Chapman, Associate Professor and Licensed Psychologist

"I met Jaydee in one of her deeper trenches and marveled at her strength, tenacity and joy in the midst of trials. Though young, she's lived a lot of life and learned some valuable lessons along the way. Reading *The Soul Grind* gives the reader a passenger seat to Jaydee's life of trial and triumphs. Her honesty, conversational style and resiliency will encourage you and remind you that you can rise from your trenches, too.

-Nika Spaulding, Resident Theologian at St Jude Oak Cliff

ISBN: 978-1-951407-41-4 Paperback

ISBN: 978-1-951407-40-7 eBook

Disclaimer

This work is non-fiction and, as such, reflects the author's memory of the experiences. Many of the names and identifying characteristics of the individuals featured in this book have been changed to protect their privacy and certain individuals are composites. Dialogue and events have been recreated; in some cases, conversations were edited to convey their substance rather than written exactly as they occurred.

Dedicated to those who got me here. You encouraged & empowered me to write, heal, feel and live.

Contents

Residue

Pictures

The photo was encased in a shiny yet antique-looking gold frame. It was collecting dust in a lit display case in the hallway outside my parents' bedroom, where all our family photos rested. They're probably just like the photos you have on your walls or by your bedside—photos you barely look at anymore, that you may knock over as your arm flails, hitting your alarm clock's snooze button for the umpteenth time. You glimpse a memory, get a bit of dust on your fingertip and then carry on with life.

This particular photo is of my two sisters and me on a rock in Hilton Head, all dressed up and grinning, with waves crashing in the background. We were so young, full of laughter and innocence. We thrived in our time together, as a family who thought we had no worries.

"Dreamy" is what I would call it if it were a song. I was such a bright-eyed, loving, joyful little girl in this picture.

The picture is a memory that gives me a burst of childhood joy, and there aren't many of those left. It was taken in a time when my dad was my superhero and my mom was an angel. I was sacred and loved and I got away with everything because I was "Jaydee Baby." My two older sisters were blissful and content and we were taken care of. All our needs were met. Happiness was the icing on our beautiful life.

Hilton Head was our long summertime tradition where we felt lighthearted and close, even on the rainiest days. We spent our time there canoeing, soaking up sunshine on the beach, giggling our way through afternoons under a tree, eating scoops of cold, drippy ice cream and whatever else we wanted.

I would pretend to pedal on the two-seater bike I shared with my dad, only moving my little legs when he glanced back at me. The wind blew my long blonde hair as I enjoyed my dad doing all the work. The rest of the family rode along, sweating and building calf muscles. I was the youngest. I was adored and spoiled and special.

I shake my head over the dusty photo. Our childhood selves were so beautiful in this sunlit memory, but sadly, unknowingly, we were on the edge of watching our family fall apart.

I don't remember looking at those photos much after the sunlight started to fade. And they look so different now.

I was a pretty darn cute kid in those pictures. I was still cute in my adolescent days, squeezing into tight, shimmying dresses with my hair jet-black, tan skin caked with makeup, sneaking out to make all kinds of a numbed-out mess of myself.

Those were the days when I began wanting nothing to do with the light and warmth in this dusty glass memory, the light that fell so dishonestly on this family full of shadows and pain.

Before You Trudge

We all have trenches. Trenches are the most raw, painful, pain-inflicting, strenuous and fiercely beautiful chapters of our lives.

2

They are the most telling parts of our journey. In this book, I dig into the "in-betweenness," the parts that are between where I was and where I am. That in-betweenness is where we become, and that's what this book of my life is all about.

The trenches are where our stories, our self-discovery, our fight for our lives and for who we are intended to happen. Our experiences trudging through them tear us down and then they make us, they mold us and they build us back up.

When we speak bravely about our trenches, we honor the warfare we've survived to live and to thrive within our souls. Why would we get to the end of each struggle, get that long-awaited breath of love, hope, light and success and not honor the spirit that brought us here? I visit my trenches often. I don't stay. I go to understand and get to know them more deeply. I love on the pieces of myself that were torn, abandoned, broken, abused and bruised and I set them back with a purpose.

I visit them to write this—for me and you.

I visit to learn, to gain wisdom and hope, to feel again with purpose. I visit to answer some of the questions I shoved away, numbed myself against or avoided for many years, so today I can connect my dots. I visit to bring truth from the deepest and darkest depths of my sorrows and my pain and my moments of surrender so that maybe you won't feel alone within yours. This journey, radically tough yet liberating, has allowed me to know and understand myself more fiercely and intimately than ever before.

This book is not pretty, it's not colorful, it's not lively in a "hype you up" way. When writing it, at times I thought "Is this too dark?" or "Do I need happy or light-hearted pauses?" and "Will this be too tough to read?" We get like that. Right? We feel our depression is boring and our voice will rattle people after we have been silent for so long. We fear others may feel small or make us feel small when they read it. We feel we can't honor our journeys by sharing them because it may make us feel too "in our stuff" about what happened back then.

We keep our truth out of the light. We hush up because of the feelings and the judgments of friends, family, previous relationships or even just "run-ins." This was foremost in my mind starting this book and writing about my father. That's been tough. We are told to glorify some figures in our lives. We are told to give their behavior a pass because "that's just how they are" or "that's all they know."

Well, in unlearning damaging rules and norms and reexamining our stories, in healing and transforming in our trenches, we get to re-wire, to re-write, to transform the pain we endured, to choose our futures, to live, breathe and behave differently.

We don't have to re-enact our trauma and the cycles we were enmeshed in. By assembling the pieces of our puzzles, getting in touch with what shaped us and surrounded us, we can choose what we want to carry with us. We can see what we know is a part of us and then choose not to let it drive us. I've revisited my life, trudged in my trenches, to discover myself on a level that lets me go forward knowing what built me—and that allows me to freely and intimately realize who I am and why I am this soul. It allows me to be passionate about who I choose to be.

This is my story, through my lens and my lens only. I'm choosing to be completely unapologetic within it. It may make you uncomfortable. If so, this is a chance to examine your story, your feelings and ask yourself what is coming up for you. If you feel emotional, submerged in all the feels and see yourself within my trenches and voice, know you're not alone. I wrote this so that you could connect your dots and experience those feelings. Allow yourself to hear them as they rattle and rise within you. Maybe even take note of what shifts for you. Whatever it is may need your love and attention.

These are my trenches, my soul grind—my journey of

grinding with my heart and soul to embrace my resilience and carry on trudging through my healing. But you've been through trenches, too. And every time I paused and avoided writing my story, I thought of you. I imagined you with this book in your hands, weeping in a crowded, buzzing coffee shop. I thought of you bringing up this book in therapy. I imagined social workers, case managers, friends and therapists using this book to help guide challenging conversations. I imagined hurting girls sitting in the window at rehab or journaling and reading at the end of the night at their residential care and mental health facilities. Maybe you're feeling stuck in a box you don't fit into, sitting in the darkness of your bedroom, yearning to be seen and heard and understood. I thought of the women in their tubs late at night trying to wash off all their pain, feeling used, abused and abandoned, soaking and scrubbing to try to feel clean again. And I thought of the women staring into their mirrors, hearing other voices in their heads, voices that deny how uniquely beautiful they are. I imagined women who haven't found their roar, finally feeling their voices tremble and their power rattling them to speak their truth after finding power in my words. I never stopped writing because I felt you waiting for me to finish.

It was tough at times to not sugarcoat, especially parts about people who should have been dear to me. I focused on chapters of my life I hadn't yet honored or truly and honestly revealed. In this process, both the hurting, angry, rebelling teen and the loving, innocent, optimistic little blue-eyed girl within me are feeling more seen and heard than I could have imagined before beginning. I'm showing you the self-discovering and growing woman within me broken open and presented boldly as I reacted to the life and relationships and environments around me.

Without sugarcoating, these are raw and real and hard truths and chapters of my journey.

Survivors, this may trigger you. So, I wrote it in short sections with many good stopping points. Pause when you need to. Dog-ear that page to come back when it gets too close to home and know these pages can wait for you to pick them back up with coffee in hand or to read them within the safety and support of a group of other bomb, resilient souls. Read this book when you're ready to look at your shadows, to feel the similarities between my journey and yours and choose to read it when you're able to be present, full of grace and love for yourself and bursting with the eagerness to rise.

Begin to Dig

Take a moment and think of yourself running freely. There are no distractions, no stops, nothing weighing you down—there's just a clear finish line ahead and nothing in your way. You can see your progress, how far you have come and how far you have to go. Seeing your progress makes it that much easier to keep going, empowering you to make it to the finish line. You finish, breeze past the banner and breathe in your success. You made it. But you never doubted you would.

Now imagine you are in muck, the deepest muck you can imagine. It feels like you're sinking in mud. It's caked to your body, relentless and heavy. You trudge doggedly through this muck, fighting the weight, pouring all your energy into making strides, into feeling a bit closer to the grass you hope is on the other side. You have no idea how far you have to go and exhaustedly, painfully, you feel you have made no progress. There's no end in sight, no light in sight. Sweat and tears are pouring from you. Your muscles are weary. And for what? You feel as though you are right where you started.

In both these scenarios, you are trudging, but in which one do you feel you are exerting more than the other? Which do you feel is demanding more strength, mental capacity and whole-hearted energy? The muck. In the muck, you are the bravest and the strongest you will ever be. You fight, you search, you connect with yourself, you fall, you fight and show up for yourself more than you ever have. You may not see or feel your power while you're in the trenches, but oh, how this muck transforms and forms you in a way you cannot even fathom.

The trenches are your soul's battlefield. It's a fight for your freaking glorious life. The trenches become the stories we carry with us, even when the muck fades and we feel cleansed, free from the chapters and moments of our journey that once suffocated us. After these trudges, we see differently, we live differently, we feel differently, we love and breathe differently, we desire to be who we were intended to be within the core of our being. Our trenches give our lives powerful, resilient, divine meaning.

The trenches are the true soul grind and you're about to be all up in mine, so get ready to grind.

2

How We Began

Dad and Mom

It all started in a Pizza Hut.

Dad was coaching college football and Mom was a nurse for the team. They hadn't actually met, but friends fixed them up on a blind date.

His family was Catholic, lively, open, loving, loyal, always up for a good time. They took you for who you were and accepted, forgave and forgot. He was the footballer, the coach, the tough guy who didn't let anything take him down. He was also the guy who struggled with behavior and grades, kicking it socially more than he did academically, at times in the wrong crowd, ultimately limiting his opportunity to play. He always carried that disappointment and those regrets. He loved sports.

Her family was Baptist, meek, conservative and private. My mom was quiet and angelic, but also a boss lady of a nurse, taking care of herself and her own home.

Her family didn't much go for this aggressive, blunt, dominant guy. Even when my parents were together, he was living a lifestyle her family didn't care for.

His family felt he was trying to be someone he wasn't for her. In that big open family, he was the only secret keeper.

The one thing these two very different families agreed on: they didn't like Mom and Dad together and didn't feel the relationship would work.

Mom and Dad heard all the advice and decided it would be great for them to get hitched anyway. It was the "hot mess no one agrees with this express" before they even said, "I do."

All the things people think will change when you put a ring on it didn't. My mom was in love with Jesus and my dad was in love with booze. They were constantly at each other about X, Y and Z—about something, anything. In less than two years, they were divorced.

Then they were like "Let's try this again—let's get back together." They decided to try to make it work. Things had to change. After going with my mother to church several times, trying to appease her and her family, Dad found Jesus. He was a "go big or go home" type of dude. He wore a suit and tie, sang all the songs and put his partying days behind him. He committed to church, was baptized, became a deacon and eventually went to seminary and pursued becoming a preacher, the real deal. He seemed to be a changed man.

So, the fallen marriage was reborn into a more cohesive one. They were going to try to make things work for the long haul this time. So, there they were, two complete opposite humans putting a Band-Aid over a hella big wound that was infecting both their souls and their environments.

And they decide to create a family. Three bomb little girl babies appeared in quick succession.

Shortly after I was born, my father got a job at an insurance company in Louisville, Kentucky. His family was in Indiana. He didn't mind jumping ship, beginning a new life. His motivators were money, Jesus and popularity and he could find those anywhere.

My mom was only 17 when her dear and sacred mother

passed. Mom is one of four and talks about her childhood with a beaming smile, saying, "I was spoiled rotten." She was the baby—unexpected. She speaks of her mother and father as if they were angels, full of humility and gratitude for their love and her family. She embodies everything her family represented, including an intense discomfort with expressing herself when her life was not what it appeared to be. She was never comfortable speaking up or causing a rumble. She was a people pleaser, didn't see why people fought and loved the Lord enough to feel submission to her husband was a reasonable way of life. So, she chose to keep her vows and move away from Tennessee, her family and all she had ever known.

She was homesick before she even left.

Jaydee Baby

After we moved, my sisters were back in school and my mom was left alone to discover this brand-new world. My dad went to work, leaving her in lonely, unknown territory. I was only weeks old. It was just us. When the house got quiet and her unhappy heart and mind began to wander, I was there. I became her safety, her companion, as we got lost all over the city. I was also her sounding board—hearing about all she was seeing, hearing, wondering and discovering for the first time as I drooled and cooed at her from my car seat.

I was their last baby, the last time anyone would do their "firsts." I was last to roll over, crawl, walk. My first words were the last first words. I barreled through all these firsts with bold excitement and then went out into the world ready to be first there, too. At the pool, I was the first to introduce myself and hear the life stories of the other little humans with their floaties. I was the first one on any dance floor, first to feel all the free and fun energy wherever I was. I loved everyone. No one was a stranger. Everyone was my friend. And I felt like a princess within my family's realm.

My dad and I were quite the pair. He called me "Jaydee Baby" and to him, I could do no wrong.

In the evenings, Dad would braid my hair and let me cuddle up in bed with him and my mom to watch endless cartoons. He would tickle and be goofy with me and on my sickest days he would camp out on the bathroom floor with me, all night if he had to.

"Sing, Jaydee Baby," he would say to me, and when I did, he'd say, "You've got a gift. You could sing professionally. I can see it now." And I would sing for my dad—Christian songs, songs that made him happy and proud. From Day One, I wanted to make sure he was proud of me. And when I disappointed him, it sunk heavily into my big-hearted and loving core. I was a big feeler. I've always felt my feelings massively. When he was disappointed, it felt like a part of me was missing. I felt my dad as a force and energy of safety. I never thought, under his watch, anything bad would happen to me or my family.

#7 with Ketchup Only

My mom was my comfort, my warm hug and my soft place to land. She sang me a song every night and she rubbed my back. She told me she sang the same song her momma sang to her. And every night before falling asleep, I wanted her to tell me a story about her life, her mom or me and my sisters when we were little. She never didn't have a story for me. She used to tell me I was the best back scratcher in the world. She also held my hand until it outgrew hers and every single time would ask, "You know what I love most?" And I would smile knowing she was going to say, "It's holding your hand in mine."

Kindergarten ended at noon each weekday, with me looking forward to seeing my mom's glorious face in the driver's side window when she swung by to get me and then we'd drive through McDonald's. When we got home, I would pour a massive amount of ketchup on my plate, sit on the carpet in front of the television and we would religiously tune in to *Happy Days* and *Mister Rogers' Neighborhood*. We called this our special "mother's days out."

We would watch our shows until it was time for my nap. Then she would wake me up from my nap and put my annoyed and rumbled little self in the van to hop in the carpool line and pick up my sisters.

While I was still waking up, my middle sister would leap and crash her wild self into the car and tell mom she lost her sweatshirt and sweatpants somewhere in the school again. She had a habit of leaving stuff everywhere but in her backpack, as she tended to pay much more attention to people than things. While mom reprimanded her for this "for the 1000th time," my older sister recounted her valorous day of academic success.

As we grew up, we had weekly rotations of who sat in the front seat—and when you sat there, you also said the prayer on the way to school. And that week you were the one who got to pick the "yummy cereal," which was our sweet option for school mornings.

Each night my dad would come home and loosen his tie. Mom would be setting the table while we waited for him to head back downstairs in his comfortable clothes to enjoy a sit-at-the-table dinner and chill for the evening.

Daddy/Daughter Days

We each had daddy/daughter days when we got to pick the place and have Dad all to ourselves without our sisters butting in. My parents were usually strict about not indulging us, never saying yes to random toys in stores and other senseless purchases, but on daddy/daughter days, there were no price tags, no limits on sugar and sweets and no "no's." Those days were the best.

On one daddy/daughter day, I often chose the theme park in our city or the zoo. Normally, we did not play the cash games between the rides, but on our day, we stopped at all of them and I always walked away with a stuffed animal—like the dolphin I cuddled each night for years. And while on most days we would walk past the gift shops, we knew we would be going in during daddy/daughter days .

Our birthdays and Christmas had the same rules. He was so strict, but on those days, we called the shots and we looked forward to them every single time. We leaned into the "yesness" of the day and gloried in all the special treats. We picked the restaurant and what we wanted to do, and he would shrug his shoulders, smile and say, "It's Christmas. You do what you want." Or "It's your birthday. You choose!"

My dad played and smiled and had bright blue eyes that looked into us and made us feel instantly like queens and at home. He was a source of strength and protection, but we also knew we were his biggest weakness. If we caught him at the right moment, during a kids' movie that tugged at his heart underneath his armor, we would catch a teary eye. He was our hero, my hero.

VeggieTales

After moving to Louisville, my parents got involved in a Christian church, joining Bible study groups and couples' groups, sending us to Sunday school, building a busy social circle for all of us. And because my father had both a driving love for religion and a will to succeed in business, he decided to make his mark by purchasing a Christian bookstore and later opening another.

These became the family business. My parents worked endless days and I spent many, many hours within the walls of the two store locations, usually cuddled up in a bean bag on the floor in the kids' section. The corner felt like a kids' wonderland—perfect for kiddos my size to watch episode after episode of *Veggie Tales*. And the bookstore felt like home. When the door opened, I'd hear my mother greet a customer with a smile in her voice. My father walked around in a suit and tie—he always wore a suit and tie—talking with other customers. Visitors perused the huge selection of Christian books my mom had arranged artfully on tables and shelves.

Business boomed. Our stores were blowing the other Christian bookstores out of the water. But as we got older, we wanted to do activities and sports rather than sit in the corner of the store watching *Veggie Tales,* so our family time started to unravel. I was getting picked up late from school. We were too stretched out as a family, so my parents accepted one of several offers on the stores.

The offer was for a life-changing amount of money. Everything changed. When the sale went through, we went to Hilton Head for an entire month.

We got rid of the old, faded, dented and scratched van that barely worked and picked out a new van that looked to my young eyes like a gold-dusted spaceship. It was honest-to-God gold and the interior had carpet and wood and leather captain chairs and lights and a TV! Later, I would hate how it stood out from the sleek luxury sedans in front of my private school and beg my mother to park far away and let me walk to school. But when we got it, it was just another canvas for my busy imagination.

We frequently visited the construction site of our massive new home and witnessed it being built from the ground up— giant beams holding a home we could all be in and never see one another. I walked its grounds with my dad. I danced and sang in this wide-open house, standing tall with its so-high ceilings. We would play on rubble and dirt hills or escape to the huge back yard, as I would stand singing, imagining myself in my gown and long flowing hair, on top of a huge pile of dirt that was most definitely my castle, waiting to be rescued by a knight in shining armor.

After it was fully framed out, I saw my mom standing in the beams of our home and I knew she already could imagine it all finished. She had a gift for seeing it before it even existed. And what she was seeing was loud, sophisticated, classy and bold.

One day, as we walked through the newly dry-walled space that was taking shape, I looked around for a place for myself. I excitedly hopped into the downstairs closet and said, "This is my room!" My mother laughed because she knew I loved even the thought of that.

If the gold spaceship parked in front didn't say loud enough that we had just landed in a lot of money, this house did. The walls were coated in silver and purple diamonds and bright yellow and white stripes. The living room and hallways were in bright yellows and reds and the backsplashes cascaded in art and checkers with different accent colors. And yet, somehow it flowed seamlessly and had visitors eager to see what was next, to explore the surprising details of my mom's decor.

My sisters and I got to pick everything down to the cushions on the window seats and photos on the walls. It was so exciting and overwhelming that I couldn't decide what mine should be. The day the painters were coming I had to finally choose—and I settled on apple green with green carpet on the floor.

We prepared to leave our small house in the neighborhood that was a community, where kids of all ages and stages met in the streets to share life and experiences. It was open and playful, and we could go to our neighbors anytime to play Barbies or sing Britney Spears on the swing set or wander our way from grass yard to grass yard. There was a baseball field in the back of our house, and on Saturday mornings, we were surrounded by laughter and cheers and announcements over an intercom.

All the rules were different where we were going. Everyone in our new neighborhood and community looked, dressed and acted the same. Not much room for scruffy clothes, Barbie and Pokémon parties. No room to just be messy in our own ways. The new neighborhood was a wealthy and older subdivision. We went from playful to proper, from dirty knees and dogs barking because we walked right up to the neighbor's home to feeling like we shouldn't dirty things or make a mess. There was lots of land, deer frolicking in the flawless landscapes, each of which could have been on the cover of a magazine. A train made its way around our home, its lonely whistle sounding throughout the night—a new and strange sound that reminded me that everything was different, that everyone in my family was further apart in this new house than we had ever been.

In the East End, the ritzy part of the city where we now lived, there were expectations, uniforms we had to wear at our new private Christian school, weekly chapel and Bible class to attend. The whole thing. We had to sign a contract not to drink. We went to church on Sunday. Period. No discussion. One time, my sister didn't feel well. As we filed out to go to church, she lay in bed, curled up in her pajamas and my mind was just blown that she wasn't going to church. Uh, she gets to stay at *home*? It was so weird because we always went. It was just what we did.

I saw my mom and dad more now that they were not at the stores. My mom could pick us up in the carpool line because my dad was the breadwinner. After living off the income from the sale of the bookstores for a while, he started looking for jobs and got into fundraising. He was great at it— building connections and getting money from people.

Even by the standards of our privileged neck of the woods, we had the "ideal" family. Parents were involved in our schools, we had private education, we were religious as f, we had bomb manners, we did not run down the aisles in church, we took notes on the sermons and did not utter a word while the pastor preached; if there was a single word or giggle, we'd get "the look," the one that said, "Get it together—now." We were always covered in bows and curls.

My oldest sister was the mature one, the momma hen, the good one. Rule-breaking was simply not in her blood and she def didn't approve of me and my sister tackling each other and arguing a bit too loudly, especially since this echoed in our connecting "Jack and Jill" bathroom. She just wanted us to get along and make good decisions. She set the bar high. Academically she was the star, valedictorian and top of her class. She sacrificed her social life for a serious scholarship, prestigious internships and a boss lady media and broadcasting job.

The middle sister came rumbling after, a physical force we heard racing around the house and speeding up and down the stairs all day. I felt her as a steady presence in my life, the mediator, never wanting to choose sides and always the voice of calm and reason when things got rough. Academics were hard for her, but she kept trucking. I never saw her give up on anything, not one thing.

She was my dad's fave. He was deeply invested in nurturing her athletic talent and made sure she made it to all kinds of camps and training opportunities. He was going to make athletics her gateway to success whether she liked it or not. We were all athletic, but she was definitely the family sports star, the speediest and a hurdler shattering records. She was a stay-at-home kind of girl and did not venture out and about much socially until she was in high school. She never got in trouble, maybe because I was causing enough ruckus for the both of us. And she was annoyed constantly about how badly I wanted to be her friend and all up in her business.

Then there was me, "Miss Where's-The-Party-At?!" Academics, no thanks. Social life, yes, please. This social butterfly had no idea why mathematics was a thing, nor did she care.

I was the rebellious life-seeker, the reckless one and the one with the extremely big heart. I thought I could be all things. I was limitless—"I'm going to be a skater that also draws that is a singer and can also be a teacher." In my mind, there wasn't anything I couldn't do.

My mom was very encouraging. She was the first to celebrate me and even once twirled me around the kitchen when I got a D in math since we celebrated anything above failing. She was the one who took me to every event, every sport and every tutoring session and sat in the car waiting for me to fall into the seat crying or to hear me celebrate some area of growth or hard work.

My mom, my dad, and my sisters—to me, they were the most perfect image of family. It felt so real to me; it was so beautiful to the little version of me.

3

The Rattling

Money made life easier, gave us comfort and shiny, expensive things. It also made us fit within a certain class and environment and opened doors to certain groups and social circles. It was all wonderful, but also, hard to let go of when the money disappeared.

When my dad sold the stores, it was to a man he trusted. He was proud to be able to take a chance on him and agreed to a structured sale, with my dad keeping responsibility for the lease on both locations. The new owner wasn't half the businessman my father was. Sales plummeted and the stores crashed. The new owner declared bankruptcy and was unable to pay the balance of the sale, which meant the payments we were living on stopped cold and left him with thousands of dollars in debt.

But the bills didn't. And neither did the need to fit in, to keep up, to paint a happy face on our fancy new crumbling life.

Our lives began to drastically change, falling apart in a sudden and completely abrupt way. We couldn't afford the house, the private education or the van. But my father wouldn't give up the things or the standing in church and community that came with them. Nobody knew how bad things were.

The main loss should have been a financial one, but that ended up being the least of what we lost.

Ultimately it was not the money that broke my father—I truly believe it was his disappointment in human nature, in himself. It was pain, grief and shame that came with trusting someone and the weakness he felt from having been taken advantage of. He trusted the man who bought the stores, and it broke him. He thought he made a really good decision and put his family in a really good place, and he was let down.

They were financially unstable—they were crashing—but they didn't tell anyone and continued to live the same life... the house, the private schools and everything. Only now he had debt and didn't know how he was going to pay it. But the most bruising and punishing for his pride was knowing it was his trust and his judgment that paved the way for this disaster.

Within a year, the deal that was supposed to make our family rich had been deemed legally unsavable. And a paper signed in trust began the unraveling of what might have been.

This feeling was far more painful than any negative in a bank account—he felt like a fool.

It could have been an opportunity, a time to heal, a time to dig, to connect his dots—the ones that led to the feels that ignited him and tormented him. He could have grown in the midst of these painful times. It could have been an awakening and a time of growth, humbling him and showing him what to do next with what he still had—his family.

But we were not enough to prop up such fatally wounded pride. He needed pride in his work, in his success, in the eyes of others. To him, our family was that picture in the golden picture frame, in the big new home—only what was seen in that privileged glow, only what society wanted to see, what he wanted society to see.

The Fairy Tale Fades

Unlike the new house's firm foundation, on which I danced many days in my innocent awe of the creation of our new space, our family was cracking. And the fault lines were breaking up my young life just as I was making my tracks out of childhood.

The house that once held my young imagination and free spirit became the place where I sat trying to figure out what becoming a woman looked like by watching my sisters intently, even when they were annoyed by me. I would come into their rooms when they came home from nights out with friends and look at their one-hour Walgreen photos, imagining myself in them. I asked many, many questions and took in their expressions and words, latching onto any scrap of feeling a part of that world. I watched them learn how to be women, and I clung to their examples.

The house also held a father who was trying to hang onto control for dear life. Despite the failure of the stores, he did not let go of the house, the school, any of it. And, always strict, his determination to keep up appearances and cover his own shortcomings intensified. And it was on a direct collision course with me, with the Jaydee that was growing and becoming and discovering my own feels and my own rhythms and my own way of being in the world.

But being ourselves wasn't okay. We had to be proper and have perfect manners. We were not to have opinions, at home or in the new Baptist church we joined after we moved into the new house. At the Christian church where I had spent my younger years, there was music, dancing and puppet shows. As my father "got religion," he had decided to go to seminary to become a preacher and started working at the seminary, which meant we had to move to the Baptist church and immerse ourselves completely in the Baptist community.

For me, it felt like having my identity locked up. When I

started to become my individual self, to express myself, to look different or act differently, I felt like I really didn't belong. It was the same at our private Christian school.

Every Sunday morning, my father would yell at me to get in the car and go to church. And I was always the last one to get in the car. I was going through those early tween and teen ages where I could never figure out what to wear. And I never felt like I looked right. It was not that I purposely made the family late; I struggled to find my place within my own clothing and to understand who I was supposed to be and appear to be in them. I either didn't look right for church or I didn't look like myself. I was flustered every time I had to face that Sunday morning mirror.

Letting out the Pain

The first time I cut, I was 13. I was sitting on my shaggy green floor with the apple green walls in the darkness, with the evening light showing through my blinds. I normally got carpet burns on my elbows from doing all my work on the floor, laying on my belly propped up on my elbows. There were books, papers and pencils sprawled out on the floor around me. I was tired. I was mad and I was stuck in this sadness that was really hard to get out of. I blamed myself for not being able to figure out my life and my family, for not being able to turn it around or fix it.

In that moment, I chose to punish myself. I also chose to feel something besides what was within me. I headed to my bathroom and I grabbed a razor. I didn't know what I was doing; I just knew I didn't want to sit with "all of this" inside me. This was the first night I cut myself, the first of many nights.

That first night I felt both relief and absence from pain. It didn't hurt and I believe it's because all of me walked around in pain every day. This was nothing. I began to wear bracelets and long-sleeved shirts and sweatshirts, and eventually just moved to my thighs and legs. It was never for attention. My body felt it had to have this escape, this "way out," this distraction from the heaviness and the depression that followed me like a dark cloud and felt like 10,000-pound weights attached to my back.

I would climb into the shower and weep as I saw the blood fall into the tub, and I would feel the sting of the aftermath. I didn't feel good enough and it seemed like this would make me stronger.

Suck it Up

We were not allowed to cry in public. He would yell at us in the car and then we had to get out with dry eyes and straight faces. At the first sign of a single public tear, he would yank me into the bathroom or grit his teeth and say, "Suck it up."

We were supposed to be poised, obedient girls. We were not allowed to wear makeup or two-piece bathing suits until we were 16. Same thing with pierced ears.

I wanted to be bold, brave, independent and wear what I wanted to wear, dang it. I fought my mom's no-two-piece-swimwear rule so hard that when she sewed a tankini together, I slowly tore it apart until it looked like I had created a new style of swimwear. The fabric was barely hanging on to cover half my belly button.

I was advocating to be a feminist when I didn't even know what the word meant. I wanted to be who I wanted to be and right then I felt like a tethered together bathing suit because none of what I was forced to wear made me feel like the girl I wanted to be. Every aspect of my life felt like that, like it was being torn and sewn back after trying to get free.

Sis Number Two used to thank me for all my nonsense and for constantly getting in trouble because it made it much easier for her to escape his attention.

But not always.

One rainy day, I was riding with Dad in the gold spaceship to pick her up at track practice. I saw her laughing and puddle-jumping through the rain-splattered window. She looked so happy, so carefree, but I saw the scrunched scowl on my dad's face, and I knew she was in for it. His face was straight terrifying. Completely oblivious to his anger, she hopped in the van, her face glowing with the most radiant childlike delight I had ever seen. In a split second, the van rattled with his rage. He shattered the joy she carried into the van, darkening it with "Didn't you even think? You could have tripped, could have ruined your whole season!" and "Stupid" and "Irresponsible" and "Don't let me ever catch you doing that again!"

I sat silently watching her glowing self slowly sink and hunch into her seat, anger and sadness visible across her body as we sat wide-eyed, shocked and trying not to make eye contact. Just moments earlier I had seen her out the window and marveled at the joy and laughter shining from her. I had wanted to hop out and join her and then she was hunched there, the interior ceiling lights of this ridiculous spectacle of a van shining on her sopping, anger-soaked face.

There had always been hints of the volatility, the anger, but now it was like a time bomb ticking constantly and we began to move on tippy-toes not knowing when it might go off.

My oldest sister heard it but had not encountered the full continual force of his verbal hits, his voice rattling the walls, because she was all that—the poised, modest, obedient super-achieving valedictorian. She set the standard for when we would be allowed to make the leaps into young womanhood, the makeup, the two-pieces, the relationships and for the face we would present in school.

But I felt like I was in a box and I wanted to box out and be heard and be different.

Jaydee to Jade

I thought when I was in high school that changing my name from Jaydee to Jade would officially excommunicate and break off the association between me and my dad.

I was named after him.

I hated carrying around what felt like this direct correlation and association with a man I wanted nothing to do with.

Jade = whoever I wanted to be.

I felt removing him from my name would also remove the pain, the hurt, the barriers, the yelling and honestly the only thing I felt I had over him...the only thing I could control. Some of my dearest friends called me Jade and it feels like love and loyalty since they trudged with me through my hardest times and still love me.

But to others and from others, it eventually came to represent a lot of pain, the name of a girl so very lost and yearning for something or someone to find and fix her.

Breaking the Mold

I often say we all had a different father. Biologically we all have the same father, but we were each raised by an entirely different man.

My dad's addiction began to flare when I was about to enter high school. He had always been inclined to it, but pills prescribed after back surgery gave him an efficient means to numb the emotional pain that was far greater than the pain caused by the incision and the staples.

By that time, my eldest sister was off on an academic scholarship to college. Number Two was slaying it athletically for our high school. She also was struggling academically. This was humbling for my father. He struggled with us having areas we needed extra support and love in. He needed us to be perfect and up to his standards. He saw us as lazy and making excuses instead of simply needing some extra time and space to work on things. He would rather have seen us as lazy than flawed, rather let us flap in the wind than ask for support. In a meeting at school, he attributed my missed classes and low scores to being lazy, rather than admitting that I was having academic trouble. The reality of us was not good enough for his picture-perfect family.

Thankfully, my mom was gifted with incredible patience.

My sister fought relentlessly for her education. She worked constantly to maintain her grades while being a track star and practicing constantly, both at school and with my dad. He had become her self-appointed personal trainer and coach, hell-bent on making her the greatest, even if she didn't want it.

I never saw anything stop her. He couldn't take the love of fun and spontaneity from her, but he picked at her, lessened her, ridiculed her, over and over. I feel like he hurt her, her brilliant smile fading, not just that day she splashed in the puddles, but so many days after that while he was throttling the life out of what she loved.

I was glad for her when she finally went off to college, even though it left me alone at home.

My dad began revealing himself at my basketball games and track meets, at business affairs and at home. He started to unload it all, publicly, uncensored and with no holding back, calling people out, refs and us particularly. My friends' fathers would pull me aside or come up to me after games to specifically acknowledge me while my dad was alone on benches more and more. Oftentimes my mom would be the only person sitting near him, since she maintained her marital responsibilities, even as she began to fade as a person.

At one point, we got an anonymous letter in the mail. The writer talked about my father's behavior, his words and loudness, and how they knew we deserved to be treated better. The letter talked about our shine and how it was dulling and how we were being hurt by his careless words and behavior. My mom tossed that letter in the fire. She couldn't deal with what would come from it.

I was running the 200 meters and 100 meters and doing the high jump on my track team. I loved it. My dad would come out to my meets and no matter how well I did, there was a "but" instead of an "I'm proud of you."

After one meet, my coach stopped me on my way off the track and said, "Jaydee, you did great today, but I think you would do better if your dad didn't come to our meets anymore."

I looked at him, surprised that he said it, but knowing what he meant.

"I just see your joy and excitement fade the minute he shows up," he added.

I shook my head, both in agreement and conflicted. I didn't want him there, but I did; I was still hoping to hear "You did a great job."

The Other Women

My dad was losing his temper more and more publicly, and making inappropriate comments about women, looking them up and down, commenting on their bodies and looks, letting his female coworkers sit in the front seat while my mom quietly assumed her position in the back. He gave them top-shelf treatment while he called his wife "the one who just let herself go" for all to hear. He talked about our mother as if she were some stranger who birthed us and us as if we were just people he was stuck with.

He would wine and dine women at work and come home and tell my mother she was fat and useless. When he was home, he distanced himself from us emotionally and mentally and when he acknowledged us, he would be yelling and screaming. Or he would ignore us, playing solitaire on his phone.

Grounded for Life

I started sneaking out my freshman year. Well, I attempted it a lot. I tried the American Girl doll under the sheets and putting tape on the door alarm to keep it from going off so I could sneak out without my parents waking up. And one night, I prepped to climb the hill above our house and get into the car of my love. He would be chilling for me in the cul-de-sac up there.

Because of my sadness, anger and rage explosiveness, my mom always let me run, even if it meant she had to take me to the gym and wait in the car. She would rather drive me than hear me explode or watch me fall into a depression. So, just in case I got caught and needed an excuse, I always slipped on my tennis shoes and crept out the door, trudging up the hill to my Prince Charming in his white Ford Explorer. He was a senior and I was the freshman who went for the athlete who would stay up long hours on the phone with me, stop and lean by my locker and let me call him obsessively 200 times.

Lordy.

Well, I trudged up the hill and got in his car and thought I had *made it*. A good talk, a good front-seat makeout session but nothing thing more. Well, I guess most people don't randomly drive in nice neighborhoods and park their cars by the curb with steam fogging the windows.

After some time, we whipped the car out and headed back to my house.

Five-thousand last kisses and a hurried nervous walk down the hill creeping back to the back yard, the grass coated in dew and as my hands slid along the wooden railing I looked up and noticed the light in the kitchen was on. Our back deck had a long row of windows that let sunshine through our kitchen and living room. And at that moment, my mother was sitting at the kitchen table with the door locked.

Yep, I had to knock on the door I left open to get back into the house I snuck out of.

Welp, that was fun while it lasted.

My mother always allowed me to run so my first instinct was to point to my dew-stained tennis shoes and let her know I was taking a late-night run—coated in Abercrombie cologne.

She wasn't buying it. She then asked me who I was with in a white Ford Explorer.

Strike two.

Uh, what white Explorer? I'm still not budging on the running.

Well, my mom had gotten a call that I was fogging up some windows in a nearby neighborhood and residents were suspicious.

I was caught.

At this point, you've caught a teen girl reeking of cologne and a great makeout session with a senior boy and the next thing you hear is *I love him.*

Lord. That about did her over.

You know what's wild, though?

I didn't lose my virginity until I was a junior in high school.

And it wasn't to my rebellious senior fling.

It was to someone else I don't want to claim, but at that point, so many people had pinned it on me and all my other friends were doing it that I thought, even if it wasn't at all the senior, that I should just go ahead and drunkenly make it happen.

4

Surprise

When I was 16, my mom suddenly announced my sisters should come home from college and we would all go out for dinner. It was weird.

As we were riding in the car together, she told us she had been seeing a therapist for quite some time and that's where we were going.

I was shocked. I felt deceived even though this was her personal healing. She was paying in cash and hiding her feelings from us. While we clearly saw the way my dad abused her, we'd only witnessed her accepting it in silence. I felt betrayed that she was healing and fighting in secret when all I wanted from her was to see it and hear it.

The therapist's office was in a tall office building with a Mexican restaurant on the first floor. We walked into a waiting room and the receptionist greeted my mother like they had spent a lot of time together. We all sat in awkward and irritated silence until Number Two and I started cracking jokes about the outdated decor.

"What is Mom making us do now?" I wondered and I could see by my sisters' expressions that they were wondering, too.

A pasty, white-haired man finally came out and brought us into his office. It seemed he already knew our names and the inner workings of our world.

We went into his office. There was a huge window through which I felt like I could see half the city. We sat down and faced him. Mom was comfortable with him, though also uncomfortable and nervous about what we were going to hear.

"Have you told them?" he asked my mother.

"No." She shook her head. She looked at us and then back at him.

"Your mom's been seeing me for a while now and we've discovered some things about your father," he said.

He looked around at us. We didn't move.

"It's going to explain a lot of what's been going on in your family, his moods, his anger, the…" He looked at my mom and she nodded. "The mistreatment."

Tell us already, I thought. Like yeah, bro, we live in it. Is there something we don't know you would like to say?

"We've discovered that he's addicted to prescription pain pills."

I had this feeling he was telling me something I already knew. I looked up at my sisters. We all just stared for what felt like a very long time, putting things together in our heads and trying to reconcile a ton of internal conflict, but it felt awfully right. We all looked back and forth at each other trying to gauge the feels, emotions and reactions of the others.

He brought out a bunch of medical papers compiled from various pharmacies and started writing on his whiteboard as he said, "We're here to talk about the impact on your mother and what we can do, what you all can do together, about this crisis."

It was so weird to sit there listening as someone we had just met tell us about our own father. It was weird that he knew far more about the situation than we did. As he was talking, we were trying to put this newly sprung news in context. It made sense and correlated with his behavior, but it was sickening.

It was a long session of my father's secret addictive life coming to the surface in all its messy clarity. The gist was that he was filling prescriptions at multiple pharmacies and was taking that stuff all the time.

We were overwhelmed. Caught up in the information and spiraling emotionally.

This explained the late nights, the unreasonably crazy rageful behavior, the glossy eyes and his forgetting fights I'll remember for the rest of my life. This would explain his disappearing acts at events, the random phone calls asking for him and the rage that made him want to "knock your head right off your neck."

Who even was this man?

My eldest sister looked betrayed. My middle sister was in disbelief. Mom was just sitting amidst all our feelings and I was disgusted. I had been over him for so long that what I was seeing and absorbing was tainted with and dripping in anger and betrayal and the knowledge that he needed to fix this. We couldn't. He needed to.

I heard everything they said about trying to get him to get treatment. It was as if it was from a distance. Crazy people talking about trying to get that man to do something. Some part of me hoped maybe just a little.

Afterward, my mother's best friend met us at a restaurant. We couldn't even make it through our meal. We all sat there, picking at our food, staring and questioning, while she and my mom tried to communicate with us as adults while being mindful that my sisters and I just heard revelations that ushered us into new territory, out of childhood and into trauma.

Dad's behavior had been a norm, a way of life and now it was scarier, more frightening and more of a betrayal. Pills created this monster of a man. How could he be putting things in his body that continually ruined our lives? It now felt even more selfish, even more powerful and big and overwhelming. A monster, a doctor's script and a secret and evil life. He was choosing to put a thing that caused this numbing, angry way of life into his mouth.

That night, I went to bed worried and slept with my sister. Our dad was a stranger and I didn't want to sleep alone.

My sisters went back to school and my mother and her therapist worked on a plan. And I waited.

The Walls

Our house was big, but the walls weren't big enough to escape the screaming, the suffering and the arguments. Cabinets and kitchen counters held my dad's pill bottles, but he was home less and less frequently. He was constantly traveling for his fundraising work and I was glad he was gone.

When he was home, I was wary of bringing friends. It was uncomfortable, a place where conflict might erupt at any moment. I didn't want anyone to know about us, to know that for nothing or just for the slightest thing, in front of anyone who was there, my father would turn into a monster—eyes bulging, neck cords popping, screaming and spitting with rage, shaking with soul-deep anger. Everyone could feel it and most feared the weight of it within him.

But into this darkness a ray of light bravely walked, trailing the baby powder smell of childhood innocence in a home where that was long gone. She and I attended the same church. Her parents were religious. She was a straight arrow, where I was a risk-taker, a cheerleader where I was the one running with the ball. She got straight A's, never got in trouble, came from a proper, lovely upright family. Since fifth grade, she had created a bubble for me within my own home where I could still be childlike and goofy and laugh.

She knew what went on in our house. She was the first person I let see it, let see how we really lived, not the perfect picture of us that showed up at church on Sunday mornings. She saw my dad, saw his rages, saw me resent and rebel, saw my mother cower. But she came anyway. And we always had fun. There was never a dull moment—but not fun that would get us into trouble. Innocent, healthy, childlike fun. She saw, but she didn't care. She separated me from my family. On the weekends we would slumber party it up, watching *Cinderella Story*, taking selfies and crushing chicken nuggets and crinkle fries. She gave me a little sense of normalcy—I could have a friend over and have a slumber party. And she showed me the power of having a best friend.

She was there on my 16th birthday when my mom had to invite her best friend and her husband to my dance party to make sure my dad stayed in line. He was so agitated that we were all on edge the whole time. Even though nothing happened that night, I ended up wishing I hadn't even had a party. He was always a short fuse away from an explosion. And it was not only humiliating to have him go off in the midst of what was supposed to be fun and joy; it was also nerve-wracking to worry about it all the time.

She was my roadmap on days I had no idea where I was going or even if I wanted to keep going. We would talk for hours and when we were not on the phone we were hanging out at school or church. She understood me and I understood her. We talked about life on levels I felt most people wouldn't get. We talked about our trenches, together, and in a way that made us both feel we could make it through anything.

And her family was my refuge. Her parents always welcomed me into their home, loved me like their own, even as my behavior became what some would consider a bad influence.

One day, in the middle of this waiting period, she called me and said her family was moving.

No. No. No. No.

I got off the phone, sobbing and ran to the kitchen to tell my mom. I couldn't take it. My home was falling apart, my grades were slipping and now my person was leaving. The feelings were too much, and my grief pulled me to the floor with the phone still in my hand.

My dad peered over the counter and laughed. "Get up," he said. "You're being ridiculous. You're just over exaggerating."

I didn't move. I couldn't. I didn't even want to.

"Oh, come on. Get a grip." He snorted with disgust and walked out.

I glanced up. My mother was also weeping.

I couldn't "get a grip." One of the only humans who genuinely knew me was leaving. The one who validated me, heard me, loved me, laughed with me and made the days seem like sunshine when there were legitimate thunderstorms, tornado-like winds, hail and rain. She brought life back into living. Without her, did I even want to? This is when my rattling truly began. It was the push into the teenagerness and broken-openness and rage and a desire not to be seen, even though I knew I would be. I was now falling into my trenches so deeply I didn't know if I wanted to crawl out this time.

One Last Try

It took three months, three whole long months, during which I was thinking "let's just get on with this" roughly 24/7. Three months of therapist visits, three months of rehearsal and booking airplane tickets and finding a time when we could gather and do this thing. Three months of forever.

But first, we were going to give him an ultimatum.

And there we were, preparing for the conversation we hoped would change everything. We would confront him. He would go to treatment. The hell of our home would go back to well, I didn't know what. But I hoped he wouldn't be this terrifying crazy person anymore, that I wouldn't have to live in hell anymore. I also didn't think he would do it for us. But the waiting was impossible.

He came through the door in his suit and tie, drenched in sweat. His collar was loosened and his eyes foggy and glazed. He put the mail on the counter.

I was sitting on the couch and turned to lean on the back as I peered into the kitchen. My mom got up from the sofa and made her way to the kitchen to speak with him, quivering and inching her way there. In my head, her walk from the couch to the kitchen seemed like years.

All of her daughters' eyes followed her.

I was repeating the words inside my head as I stared at my mom, who was having the hardest time forcing these same words out of her lips.

We rehearsed this. We went over every possible scenario. We planned down to the syllable. She *knows this*.

Why is it so hard for her to just speak?

Her movements seemed to last forever and her words were scattered, jumbled and fear-stricken. What would happen next? Would we need to use the packed luggage in our mother's trunk or would we be laying our heads in our own beds tonight?

We hung on every word.

He was going to be willing, right? We wouldn't have to go this far, right? We wouldn't have to flee our own home, would we? We wouldn't have to shut our own door and open a motel room door because he was selfish enough to choose his pills over his family. Right?

Well, that's what my sisters thought. I was all about some pessimism. He was for sure going to make us leave and I was all for it. To be honest, I thought he should be the one to leave, but I knew he wasn't going to go anywhere, listen to anyone and I just wanted my mom to go on with the show.

It was time to confront him.

The words seemed sudden and loud when they finally came.

"You have a full-fledged addiction," Mom said.

He stared. He was abnormally calm for a man who normally walked around enraged. His speech was slow.

"What? No."

Mom's next words seemed to take forever to get out.

"Yes, we know about your addiction and all your prescriptions and either you are going to get help and leave or we are going to have to leave you."

He was sweating and his face turned red. It was as if he knew something was rattling but wasn't in the right space to connect all of it.

"No," he said. "No, it's not...I don't. It's not true."

His expression was unsettling, angry and solemn, but he was grinning like he figured he would be able to talk himself out of this one.

"Yes, it is. We know," my mother said through trembling lips.

He gritted his teeth, slammed his hand on the counter.

"You...are...not...leaving."

Then We Left

We sat in the van in the Sonic parking lot after leaving our home scattered and rushed. My mother's best friend hopped in our car and they began trying to warm up a very difficult and terrifying moment for all of us, a moment when we were all processing a solemn awakening.

We sat in the stall, holding our breath when any car came around the corner. Worry sank into my bones as I watched the reactions of my people, my family, to this new truth.

I knew life had just gotten real.

My young mind was spinning, trying to wrap itself around

the idea that I had just fled my own father, that we had packed our bags and left our home. With our father inside it. He was so obviously stoned when we left that I was sure he was still trying to untie his tie and unbutton his shirt. He was probably still standing right there and not realizing the full importance of what had taken place.

It was Wednesday. The intervention would be on Saturday. Friends and family were coming from out of town and we would stay away from the house, from him until then.

The four of us were in a motel scattered around a first-floor room. I was crouched on the floor. My sisters sat in the beds. And my mom rustled around the room. We all had our pieces of notebook paper out to write the statements we would soon read in front of our father.

"It made me sad when…" "It made me upset when…" "It made me happy when…"

The therapist told us we needed to have some positives in our letters, talking about times when he was sober, when we were happy and the memories with him we cherished.

Uh, when? I was having a really difficult time with this part. And? Why? Why do we need to sugarcoat hell? Sugar-coating and beating around the bush will make him sober? "Gotcha," I thought.

Well, I guess I was happy when you didn't yell, when you and mom had a moment of laughter, when I was able to not walk around on tippy-toes or not pace my room 50 times before I could muster up the courage to ask you something simple, like whether I could go to a friend's house or use the telephone. I just never knew what your reaction would be.

I had watched *Intervention* on TV and was drawn in and moved by the people on it and their heartfelt pleas for their loved ones to get help. It was a little different writing my own, in a motel room, for my own dad.

It was even more troubling to see my sisters and my

mother sprawled out on beds, pondering what they could say to save a man who says he doesn't need to be saved.

The next couple of days didn't feel real. It was like I was living his drugged-out life, just a big ol' blur.

It straight up felt like an episode of *Intervention*.

Except it wasn't on A&E. It was my life.

He found out which hotel we were in because of the credit card. He sat outside the hotel. I could see him through the window. I was thinking "This is so weird. Is my dad going to get us? Is this real life? Am I really hiding from my own dad?"

My mom's phone was ringing constantly. The ringtone was stuck in my head, and I heard his voice, angry, crazed on the other end. I heard voicemail after voicemail until her inbox was full of him saying, "I flushed them, I flushed them all."

I was thinking about things you never imagine wondering in a hotel room...can just anyone get in the lobby? Can anyone cancel a room? Can anyone gain access to a room? When will we ever be able to leave? Is he going to camp out there until we run out of money? I was looking at people differently, hotels differently, wondering just how many other people were fleeing from their own lives here?

I had never felt fear like that. I didn't know what he was capable of. But I wasn't afraid for myself—I was afraid for my mom. I felt like I was the one to protect my mom. And I was angry. We were fleeing from someone that was supposed to make us feel at home.

Then my father canceled the credit cards and we went to motel after motel. Mom had stashed some money and started using cash.

Thursday night, we went to a church service. I think my mother was trying to find some type of sanity and a heavenly sign of some sort. We also wanted a place to go other than a hotel room, Walmart and restaurants.

I sat in the pew, thinking about how no one else was hiding from their own dad—or were they? I looked around the church. We are living in that moment and nobody there knew what we'd been doing for the last 72 hours. That thought rocked my world—how many other people were living through this and we didn't know? We went to church, but we didn't go to school because my mom was afraid he would find us there. It was crazy. I felt like I was seeing an entirely different way of life. I felt the realness of it all and it rattled me to know there were so many more people living in this world of hurt.

I clung to being in the moment, to a feeling that "we have to make the most of right now." We went to Walmart to try on Halloween masks, laughing at all the silly looks, a release we needed so badly. We stuck together. We chose to love fiercely, laugh uncontrollably and hold sacred to one another in the midst of what seemed like the most treacherous storm.

On Saturday, we went to the therapist's office. The buttons in the elevator were oldish and black and lit up. I shook. I had not seen this man, my father, for three days, except outside motel and hotel windows, his voice echoing desperately over too many voicemails to count. This elevator captured all those feels. When the door opened, I didn't know what to expect.

We walked in to see the others who knew what had been happening and had shown up to be there for us—and for the man they once knew and still loved. We sat in the big room with the window that looked out over the town. It felt more like a meeting space than a therapist's office.

A youth minister who had supported my sisters and me through the process of the past few months and who had heard some of our grief and pain was there. And two dear friends came from out of town. Our chairs faced the chair we saved for my dad. The therapist had told us he might not go to rehab, he might not care. He prepared us for the worst knowing we hoped for the best, that our dad would leave this room and head to the airport with the bag my mother had already packed for him and go to rehab in Florida.

He walked in with a smirk and a sly laugh.

"You've got to be kidding me," he said as he scanned the room.

We went around the table and read our letters out loud. I watched him. His face remained inert, no change in expression. He wasn't going. From the moment he walked in, I think we all felt that. Everyone had seen the impact on him, on us—their friends from Tennessee, his family, friends, the church youth counselor, everyone but him.

After we read our letters, we looked at him. The therapist said, "Your family and friends are concerned about you. They love you and want to see you happier and healthier. That's what this is all about." He nodded to my mother, who produced and had paid for the airline ticket.

"I got this for you," she said. "It's to Florida. There's a place there. You can get help."

Her voice trailed off at the look on his face. He was angry and disgusted and maybe I saw hurt lurking behind the wall. He looked at us and saw a circle of disloyalty.

"Yeah. I know all about your big plans. I saw all this crap on the credit card statement. It's canceled."

"Canceled?" my mom said.

"Yeah. No way am I going to go. I'm definitely not leaving work and I do not have an issue. I'll take care of it here."

After this ridiculous, emotional, heart-rending letter-reading session, revealing and reliving years of pain and sadness, after this draining two-hour intervention, we all went to Cracker Barrel. We had lunch and tried to make chit chat.

I wondered. Who legit has a life-altering three days and then goes and gets lunch and goes back to the home we fled from? Who does this? Uh, us—this was our life.

So, that's what we did. We went back home to our lives. Nothing changed, except he got worse. And sneakier.

Worse

Having promised to handle it, he just got more secretive. He had a pill container on one side of his sink with a carefully counted number of pills. Knowing his addiction had an audience, he wanted to make sure the count on this pill bottle was correct, just enough to manage the pain from the back surgery that had gotten him started on the opioids.

But I looked out the window and saw him swallowing pills in the car. I was done. I was burning with hatred and fury and I sure wasn't going to help him keep secrets. I started calling him out every chance I got.

While I got angrier, my mother gave up. I felt like I was alone in this madhouse with a devil who used to be my father and a ghost who used to be my mother. I would not be a ghost. I was alive and burning and hurting and trying to wake her from the dead and get her to do something, to help me, to help herself.

Snapshot

My mother sat on the corner of a red flower-covered sofa, her legs wrapped to her side, a napkin in her hand and a towel draped over the side of the couch.

There was a brown, magazine-covered coffee table next to her with a lamp and phone, which was constantly on silent. We never used the landline anymore because we were always getting calls from bill collectors.

My dad was on the other side of this couch. I was in the middle, behind them, leaning on the fading couch, battling the silence of my mother and the rage of my father.

My mother was silent, broken and full of fear. I was trying to wake her up and get her warrior to rise and fight for herself, but she just didn't have it in her anymore. I was a one-woman army. I wasn't going to let her go down. I felt if I stopped, I would lose her completely.

I had found the dating sites he used on the computer and printed out his "activity."

"This is what you're doing!" I yelled at him, leaning over the sofa and waving the papers in his face. "This is why I hate you."

I wanted her to see it and react. I could not understand why she constantly sank into the couch and into her deep silence.

"Get off my account," he bellowed at me. "It's none of your business."

"Mom, why are you letting him do this?" I shrieked. "Why are you letting him talk to me like that? Speak up! Don't let him treat you like that. He's going out on you and spending money on other women while you sit here, on this sofa, like you're not even a person anymore!"

I wanted her to stand up for herself when he inched close to her face, yelling, with spit coming from his mouth while he bit the edge of his lip.

I'd had enough. I wasn't going to take it.

I had become her voice, her shield and her protector.

I didn't turn to her anymore or get tears in my eyes or feel my spirit defeated because no one was standing up or advocating for her. I just chose to do it myself.

I didn't look at her to fight for herself anymore. I began to assume she wouldn't.

And from that point on, you didn't speak to my mother that way.

And you definitely weren't going to speak to me that way.

You single-handedly are the cause of destroying my family.

It became our family portrait: my mom silent on the couch, me reckless and rageful in the middle and my dad high and angry, rummaging around the kitchen, slamming the back door in an exaggerated exit to go out for a dip of tobacco.

I said I would never be her. I would never be so submissive that I was silent. I would never allow a man to speak to me that way and would for damn sure never fail to speak up for myself or realize I was worth more.

I swore I would never allow anyone to hurt her and I would fight for her until she hurt no more. I thought my anger was working, my yelling was a roar louder than his. I thought she was feeling heard, understood and a bit stronger every time I intervened.

None of this was true.

I was just allowing all my feelings to be compressed into cold and defiant anger. The type that bit by bit hardens a once very, very soft heart and cages the ability to let love in.

The type that sees yelling as the only way to communicate.

And distances herself from all things that may bring warmth.

Searching for something that is caged is very difficult.

Smiles began to fade, people began to change, and drinking became a way of numbing what already felt numb and allowing me to disengage.

Rounds and rounds of beer pong and Heaven Hill whiskey mixed in water bottles.

Sonic parking lots where my face would go numb and I would begin to float into bad decisions and end up rummaging around at our front door for my key, where my mom accused me of drinking.

Every time she asked, I got angry with her and told her no.

I wanted to be seen and heard, yet I pushed it all away and at times convinced myself and others I didn't want any of it.

I knew how to be a warrior, but I had no other way to be.

My mom looked at me one of those nights, saying with tears in her eyes, "Where is my Jaydee? I want her back."

I looked at her and said, "You're never getting her back. She's gone."

Home

My home was my battlefield, my room where I wept and screamed and the neighborhood pavement where I released some pain as I ran and ran and ran, never escaping anything.

He started traveling and living in different places where he was working. My mom loved it—she just wanted him to be away. For me, it was an opportunity to see what I could get away with.

This was when the women started popping up—the ones he was wining and dining. And people started noticing: there was that note in the mailbox that mom burned so he wouldn't see it.

But I wasn't quiet about his transgressions. I was going to yell and scream, and he was going to see and hear me. And one night I pushed and pushed. He was stone cold, and I was cursing, escalating, knowing I was going too far. I was aiming for the normal verbal back and forth battle, but this was different. He looked different and was coming towards me and the anger left his voice, but he lost it and threw me on his and my mother's bed in a chokehold, his hands wrapped around my neck. I was screaming and looking into his high eyes, losing breath and yelling, "You're going to kill me!"

I heard my mom hurrying up the stairs with my dog following, and, for the first time in a long time, she was there. Her wounded self cracked open. I heard her for the first time rattling awake from her silent slumber and telling him to "*Stop! Stop! Stop!*" as she climbed on the bed to pull him off of me.

I jumped off the bed and ran into my room, slamming the door behind me, shaking—shaking because I could have lost all my breath and shaking because my mom stood up for me. This had rattled her out of the slumber of sadness and abuse, and I was so grateful she finally stood up to him.

My mom moved differently after this. She knew she couldn't walk away but she was going to do her best to protect me even if that meant I rarely stayed there anymore. Still, she was a silent mover. When I started staying with friends, I never knew she was talking to their parents, telling them home wasn't safe for me, begging them to keep me there, to let me stay.

5

Genes

See, my father was a lot like me and vice versa.

He was extroverted and popular, easy to grow hot-headed and quick to argue with someone until he had won. In situations that made him feel betrayed, he felt, whether it was justified or not, he had to defend himself. He fell face-first because the weight of regret and forceful blame is enough to knock someone straight out. All the things he wanted—sports scholarships, a successful business, a beautiful family—faded or crashed radically, one by one.

He made many, many "asinine" decisions. I had no idea what asinine meant or that the word existed until my dad used it about me—when I got detention, failed a test, got caught in the hallway. And we would yell at each other—cursing, rattling the walls with the volume.

Asinine? I thought. You mean like your drunken nights, running with a crowd of grown men who didn't know how to handle a gun and fired in rage instead of using words? Didn't you put socializing, girls, booze and ball over any reasonable academic decision?

My relationship with him was like dip. Yup, I'm talking Grizzly, chewing tobacco, chew, the nasty brown tub of nicotine muck that tangles up in your teeth and fills the empty bottles rattling in the car with brown spit.

When I was little, I would cuddle up in the mornings watching cartoons with Mom and Dad or hanging out on the bed if they were both getting ready for their days, and one day I was playing with their sheets and a can was wrapped up in them. Curious, I picked it up and was trying to figure it out. My dad simply laughed and said, "It's shoe polish, you know the stuff Mommy uses to shine my shoes."

I didn't realize until later in life that my dad loved him some dip and my momma hated it, so he dipped outside while taking the dog out or in the car where later he would deny that it was dip residue that was clinging to the rims of his cup holders or insist that something else remained in the crevasses of his teeth.

Our life and relationship were that straight-up dip habit— a direct refusal, even with the obvious, to be honest.

And when we had an opportunity to shoot it straight, there was a persistent and fierce resistance to opening up any portal that might bring humbling, truth-telling and healthy communication. But I still wanted it.

Stolen Truth Thunder

I had become as good as my father at keeping terrible secrets. I had been cutting for a couple of years before I slipped and my mother saw what I had been hiding.

I was 17. We were on our way to the gym when the car swerved off the road. I looked up and saw my mom's eyes well up with tears. She pointed to my wrist and pulled off the busy road into a parking lot. I had worn a short sleeve top instead of my usual long sleeves. These scars and lines were my norm. I had to remind myself to cover them up, that they would upset others. That day I forgot.

"Jaydee…" she faltered.

I just looked at her. I didn't have anything for her.

"I…" She hunched over the wheel and then looked up at me. "I love you, honey," she whispered. "Why…?"

I had nothing. I had no answer that would heal her broken heart.

"Just forget it," I said.

We sat there. I could feel her wanting an answer, an explanation, something she could understand and fix and heal. I didn't say a word.

Finally, she pulled back onto the road. The ride to the gym was quiet and I could feel the sadness of her heart, but I still didn't care to try to explain any of it.

"Listen, Mom," I said.

"Yes, honey," she looked at me, hopefully.

"Just don't tell Dad, okay? He won't understand."

A piece of me also didn't want him to think I was so down, so depressed, had gotten to the point of hurting myself because of him. I needed him to think he didn't faze me, and this showed that his impact was killing me.

She dropped me off at the gym and I cannot imagine what waiting for me in the car for the next hour was like for her.

I was not a fan of therapists. My parents constantly forced me to go. One said, "Don't bring her back. She's not talking. There's nothing I can do for her." Another died. For real. It was after my mom found out about the cutting and the therapist and I were working on the issue. The deal I had with Mom was that if I stopped cutting, I could get a tattoo. Then the therapist had a heart attack.

The next one, though, she stole my truth.

After the therapist who died, my mother made me an appointment with a new one. I rode there with my mom hoping to be able to set my truth free and maybe just maybe be seen.

I was ready to talk, ready to tell my father. I wanted to tell him. I wanted to talk to the new therapist about having that conversation with him.

But when I walked in, the first time seeing the therapist, ready to get down to it, he was there in the room already.

Without knowing me, without meeting me, without hearing from me, she had told him my "truth." My mother told the therapist and the therapist told my father. She told him I had been cutting. Alone in a room with my father, without me there, she told him.

Then I walked in and he looked at me as if I were crazy.

"Don't even say anything," he said.

I had been looking forward to looking him in the eyes and expressing what was going on in my life and she took that from me.

We were there less than five minutes and they told me I had no choice but to go to a mental health facility.

I started screaming, yelling. I fled into the grass in the middle of the office complex and started screaming, drawing people out of their offices.

My dad tried to wrangle me and all I could say was, "Don't you dare come near me."

My parents gave me until that evening to get my stuff—to go to the families I had been staying with.

My middle sister was there. She came with my mom to drop me off and gave me a piggy-back ride into the hospital, just like she had carried me through many of the hardest moments of my life. She was acting like it was going to be just fine. She was always my peace in the midst of what felt like the biggest storms. She had a fierce way of reminding me that I would be okay, I could do this—this feeling thing and this healing thing.

Dad didn't come. I told him he couldn't. No visitors but my mom and my sisters.

I had no idea how long I was going to be there.

I was feeling this disappointment deep, deep in my heart. I

was angry and I was sad that the opportunity to tell my truth myself had been stolen from me.

I was enraged, caged again and decided that from then on, no therapist's office would be a place I could be free—that none of them were worthy of seeing me.

Hospital

Author and therapist Brené Brown talks about "face down in the arena" times in life.

They're our most profoundly awful moments, the worst of our days, the days when it's hard to fathom one good moment coming or one instant of calm—times when it feels the storm is never-ending, the moments of deepest grief. It's when you feel you can't even catch a breath, when the pain that seems to never go away is felt deep in your heart. It's when you know that you're at the lowest point you could dig yourself into, but have completely thrown down the shovel, crying dirt-stained tears as you surrender to the knowledge that you don't even want to climb up...the moments when life is unbearable and there's no light at the end of this freaking tunnel and you can't seem to muster up the match within your soul to spark the flame.

That was the hospital—one of my big face down moments.

I was 17. I had been cutting for years. With my sleeves rolled up and my pants, my arms and thighs bearing witness to the pain I had been trying to get out of me.

I woke up on a cot in the hallway of a treatment facility on a 24-hour suicide watch. I was wearing green scrubs that contrasted with my bleached-blonde hair and sunburnt, tanning-bed skin.

I wasn't allowed to have any kind of laces or wiring, nothing of my own.

I was about to burst into explosive tears for the first time in years.

I was trying to muster up my angry and fierce fighting self when I realized I was surrounded by women who were face down in the arena with me.

I was lying wide awake in a cold hallway with people staring at me.

Morning seemed like it took forever to come...but it finally came.

The bathroom door was monitored, as was every square inch around me, and a loud alarm signaled the door was ajar.

Where in the world was I?

What do I even do?

Why did they just leave me here?

Why is everyone asking me why I am here?

When can I leave?

I don't deserve to be here.

The hospital had sayings—repetitive rhymes, classes, point systems, schedules and routines and people were assigned seats and trays for their food. It was like I had landed on another planet.

Trying to act like I wasn't about to fall on the floor in a terrified heap of a mess, I grabbed the first tray I saw in the cafeteria.

I felt someone sweep in behind me and tell me I had taken her tray and I had also stolen her seat.

What she didn't know was that I was about to break. The door was still propped open and the alarm sound was agitating me. I wasn't allowed any personal items. I was sent here without any warning. I spent the night in the hallway, and I had hardly slept because of the new territory and the fact my life had just flipped upside down. And my heart was about to explode in my "trying to act like I didn't care" sad, broken-souled, alone, mess of a self.

So, I glared at the girl who wanted the tray and gave her a

taste of my major don't-mess-with-me demeanor and uttered some type of rude "I don't care to take your nasty food"— tears welling out my eyeballs and with a wanting to get the F outta here snarl.

She was my complete opposite: very tall, broad shoulders, the top dog of the center. She was dark and her hair was in a badass fro. She had the same look I did, and we recognized we were in the same face-down place. She looked around and I realized that, not only was I on her turf, but also her boldness made it clear that no one was going to mess with her.

She looked at me and said, "I got your back" and I knew no one was going to mess with me either.

After that we never separated. We sat by a window looking at the cars and talked about life, why we were there and how we got there, our families, our joy and our pain. She was a poet—her words gave me chills and she encouraged me to write.

She told me what she knew about our fellow patients. She said she wished they would leave and never come back because they had so much to live for. She told me she didn't mind being here because the world outside was even worse. She was a processor and a listener. She too had a hard shell but, in her writing, I saw all her beauty and her resilience, and that she had no idea how extraordinary a soul she truly was. No one had taken the time to see past her pain or ask her why she hurt.

In the hospital, people showed their "before" photos when we met. They wanted me to see them as they looked before they were locked up. There, they felt they were disappearing. They wanted me to see the girl in the photo, not the one standing in front of me.

But they came alive talking about their dreams. Some wanted to stay; some desperately wanted to leave; others came back while I was there because, they said, their families were already sick of them.

I walked out two days later into what they call "freedom" and I had to leave her behind. The poet.

While I was face down in this arena, I looked around and saw her face and I'll be forever grateful that she honored me by her truth telling.

She spoke my language.

She resonated with my pain and my need to be heard.

She was my people.

While we were in those moments we were both able to light a match to our innate flames, which were for both of us weak at the time, and create an epic flame between us that kickstarted a light in our darkest tunnel so we could see there actually was an end to it.

I'll never forget her.

I have a journal from those days where I remember the poetry we sat and shared together that was the emptying of our souls on paper.

I hope she is somewhere out there boldly jotting down her story for the world to see how insanely brilliant a being she is and how much she is love itself.

Trudging with Jesus

I avoided the religion topic for far too long.

My upbringing has brought this hesitation.

My hesitation to judge where and what I was raised around.

Tiptoeing around a very intimate and heavy topic.

Fear of being misunderstood and rejected again.

And in all honesty, the fear of losing the humans I share to invest in: those trudging.

The real deal, authentic, surviving souls...my people.

I've had many people ask, "Where is God in your story?" And many have offered me a seat next to them in church when I began telling my story.

The truth is my religion, my belief system was rocked by the false representation of Jesus.

Mirrored by a father who would attend seminary and preach behind the pulpit and, on the ride home, verbally abuse and degrade my mother.

Mirrored by "Don't run in church" along with "Don't speak, don't swear, don't talk too loud, don't do or think," minimizing the capabilities and fierce voices of women and the innocent joy of childhood.

Mirrored by a Christian school that made me feel like an unworthy outcast.

Mirrored by individuals in church disdaining an out-of-wedlock pregnancy while passing the offering plate.

Mirrored by Christians who claim to love others yet don't offer a hand to those trudging in deep trenches.

Mirrored by me becoming one that "needed saving" but finding that no one was helping a sista out.

Mirrored by classes telling me how to live, forcing me to memorize chapters of the Bible, and ignoring my sadness, grief, and pain.

You need a memory verse? I got you.

You need a scripture to use? I got you.

You need a good sermon idea or choir song? I know them all.

Need to know how to fake it 'til you make it and learn when to raise those hands high? I got you; I know all the tricks to look the part.

You see…I stepped away from God because of what I saw people do.

Until I read the passage about Jesus investing in the prostitute.

I don't know what you all see.

But I see a God in the trenches.

Not one denying other's sacred space.

I see a God that wants you to worship with your passions and by investing in your gifts and loving on others.

I don't see a bonfire s'mores party kinda Jesus. We don't have kumbayas.

Me and God wrestle; we disagree, we argue. I warrior up, I yell, I fall to my knees, I surrender and then get back up again. I've driven the car of life and I've given him the keys. He doesn't whisper to me. He rattles my existence.

God is not always what I see in this world because I often feel we are far away from what he intended. I think God would be rattling some tables like He did back in the day as He honored his rage.

But I do see him in people.

When I have seen God is not when people invite me to sit with them at church, not when a Bible was tossed at me, not when someone said they would send a prayer up but didn't follow through.

It is when people showed up in my toughest times.

When they sat down with me or woke me from my numbness.

It's when they chose love for me instead of judgment.

It's when they welcomed me in, in my roughest.

It's when they deemed me lovable in my recklessness.

And it's when they honored my journey with my God because they knew that's how we grind and how we roll.

Just because God is not mentioned at every single post of my journey does not mean that He is not pivotal in my redemption story.

It means that I'm worshiping differently than you.

He gets it and that's all that matters.

It took me leaving all I had been taught about spirituality and religion to find it again.

6

The Fog

Junior year of high school I had a .66 GPA.

Yes, .66 GPA. Pretty sure someone gave me points for putting my name on a paper at some point.

I was caught cheating on a math exam soon after and that F would send me over the edge, both emotionally and academically.

I was drinking, going out, depressed, using self-mutilation to cope, constantly arguing and screaming with my father—and honestly anyone at this point—and was straight "out of control."

I was failing...life. Or so I was told.

The only relief I got from my rage and my sadness and the deep well of feelings that were so stuffed down that they were unknown, even to me, was when Sis Number Two was home. She would toss my shoes at me, hold me in hugs until I would burst past the rage to tears and drag me out to run up and down steep hills 'till I got what was stirring within me out.

But the relief never lasted long enough to truly heal.

If someone did something...it had to be me.

I didn't go a day without a counselor's office call or my father yelling at me.

Parents told their children I was the troubled kid.

And I was becoming a lost cause.

People were giving up on me.

Psh, I was giving up on me.

And in that space is where I did all of my decision making.

Decision Making

My life was a series of sporadic attempts to breathe and live in the midst of all-consuming trouble.

It felt like everyone was sitting at the kitchen table—not just my mom, but the entire town—waiting for me to show up have made yet another mistake.

I honestly don't know what the last straw was.

There was the time I snagged the keys from the counter and took the extra car to a nearby park, put the sunroof down, opened up my pink striped pack of cigarettes and threw on my mixed CD to meet a friend and smoke a cig. I had calculated the time down to the second, driving around the park and getting home, parking the car exactly where an oil spot hit the pavement in the driveway, catty-cornered and all. I aired out the car and went up to my room to hide out until the door clicked and daddio and my mom came back home from work. I never did get caught—may have been the only thing I ever got away with.

Or maybe it was the time they were tracking my car mileage to make sure I was only going to school and back. So I had someone meet me at the gas station nearby, on my way home, to exchange two water bottles for vodka mixes I could drink on the way to the house so that I could then pass out in bed.

When I was grounded and not able to do a damn thing, I got recklessly and numbingly creative.

Or maybe it was the time I faked going with my friends to

a university tour when really, I just had a blackout weekend and met up with my fling from freshman year.

Or maybe it was the Sonic trips where my slushies turned into hyped-up alcoholic beverages and where I finally learned you had to actually inhale the cigarette smoke to get anything from it.

Or when I was first handed a pill and realized I knew exactly why my dad liked them so much.

Or when I went to the school functions but had to bong a few beers before showing up and take a pill as I strayed back to my car while everyone else gathered around campfires.

Or maybe the time I was pretty much stalked by my school's staff and teachers at our homecoming dance. The dance was chaperoned by the staff of my private school, they had previously talked to my mom and were to report to her if I left early. The second I went into the hallway and left our school gym, where the dance was being held I was greeted by the staff that told me I shouldn't be leaving early and if I was going, I needed to call my family and tell them.

Our crew walked out and had plans for an after-party and to escape this "lame dance." My mom called and said I wasn't going anywhere and to come home. We were worried that someone would search the car, because, at this point my mom had called everyone's moms, also ruining their after-party plans.

So, we dumped the liquor into trash cans around our town. When we got to the friend's home, my friend's mom had come outside, after being contacted by my mom, and searched the car, which made me yell at her. I knew the other parents thought it was solely me causing their children to make "bad decisions."

No one wanted their children to hang out with me. I was the troublemaker.

My mom came and made me get in the car and leave.

At first my rebellion actually wasn't as bad as people

assumed. It was after the assumptions turned to judgments and the judgments turned into lack of asking and the lack of asking turned into punishment and yelling that things got dangerous and scary and toxic.

No Saviors

My life that year:

Many slumber parties gone wrong as I drunkenly said things that hurt those I loved.

Baseball games I don't remember.

Day drinking and driving under the influence.

Hanging out with anyone who wanted to enjoy a buzz at any hour.

Watching the faces of those I loved and who I knew fiercely loved me, change.

It was dawn. I was sitting by the river with my best friend at the time. I still had a good bit of booze in my blood from the all-nighter that was just ending.

"I want you back, Jaydee," she said. "The partying was fun for a while, but you're drinking too much, ya know? I want you back, sober and making sense, and really here with me, not numb all the time."

I looked at her blearily. I could hear her pain and frustration, but it was like a far distant train. And the alcohol kept me from feeling it. I just watched the water go by. That's what my thoughts and feelings were like when I was like this. They just floated by.

"I like it—I like my thoughts, my views, my life better this way," I said. "It is all better this way—no worries, no pain, no sadness, no truth, no reality. I'm just a buzz away from whatever I want it to be."

Like so many others, she loved me but had to begin to step away because it was hurting her.

It's tough to love someone in their trenches, to see them fade into rebellion, rage, numbness and grief. It's really hard realizing you can't love them enough to break them open, to show them what being in their "stuff" is not allowing them to notice for themselves or to choose to change their lifestyle for them. You can't, no matter how many times you try, make them leave an abusive partner or have them stop getting high. You can only tell them so many times that they could overdose or die or that you fear for their life and hope that will actually be the reason they re-direct their life. Some of my friends distanced themselves, others told me I was doing too much—too much drinking, too much acting out, too much getting high, too much and all at too high a volume. And some of my people continued to hang tight with me and love me through it all without judgment.

People lined up to "heal" me or to shame and abandon me.

Some wanted the gratification they would get from being a savior.

Some just talked about me behind my back.

Some chose to love me all up in them.

Some avoided all topics but the weather.

And some chose to be all down in the trenches with me because they were not ready to do any work in their lives either.

The pill poppers got high with me.

The drinkers drank with me.

The ones who wanted to save me told me they would "pray for me" or left me notes in my locker about how they were worried about me or wrote letters to my mom concerned about my father and his abrupt changes.

Others added us to their prayer chains.

Still others housed me, spoke truth to me, sat on lawns at parties and gatherings and had life with me.

Others held me and cried with me and many took me

under their wings and just straight up loved this messy and wild version of me.

You can tell where you are in life by whom you surround yourself with.

When I was "in my stuff," I blocked out and became defensive with the truth-tellers. I pushed them away, formed alliances against them. The truth-tellers were the first to go when I was not ready to grow, not ready to change my behavior, not ready to be humbled and have some very hard conversations.

My sister called me out, so I despised her at times. My mother wanted me sober and healthy and proper and I hated her for it. I wasn't ready to change, to grow, to be humbled, so I wanted nothing to do with anyone that made me look at those pieces of myself. They made me uncomfortable in my own life, made me question and wonder and feel a pit in my stomach. I only wanted to be around those who chose to numb it with me instead of feeling it and learning from it and growing.

I wanted to surround myself with those who drank, who took pills, who dressed up and partied until their faces also went numb because I knew they wouldn't judge me or tell me to stop.

There were options but I surrounded myself with people who made it easy for me to remain in my trenches and not make hard and life-changing decisions. Or not even just life-changing; it was just so difficult for me to humble myself and make amends, say I was wrong, allow others to support me and hear I needed help. I wanted to be around the people who didn't rattle the comfort I had found in complete discomfort. It felt like "they win, I lose." But I wasn't winning. I was actually desperately losing my own game.

Dead or Pregnant

It was getting dark. I hurried downstairs hoping I wasn't seen, prepared to lie about where I would be spending the next few hours of my life, in an outfit that I was sure would not be approved.

Dad wandered out of the kitchen and looked me up and down, stopping before he got to my face. He shook his head, disappointed.

"You are either going to wind up dead or pregnant," he said, shaking his head.

This exchange was our usual way of saying goodbye as I left the house. Sometimes I yelled at him, telling him he didn't know me or that I didn't care what he thought. But tonight, I was in a hurry.

I wanted to get out of the house, to be with my people, my friends. My feelings were all types of cooped up inside. The only one I could seem to shake loose at that moment was "I hate you," which is what I said as I slammed out of the house.

The Last Hurrah

The smell of fall and the crisp crunch of leaves, the hint of a bonfire and the burnt smell of campfire were heavy on my very box-dyed hair, flannels, jeans and makeup for days. I was at a friend's house, but I wasn't chasing relationships; I was chasing numbness, and we chased it all over town that night.

These were my people, but this weekend felt different.

My parents didn't seem as concerned as usual, but I still didn't want to check my phone for their usual barrage of text messages. I didn't care to see if they had asked where I was or what I was doing or demanded I be here or there. I had already decided I wouldn't care or answer. This weekend I was more determined and careless in my rebellion, and less worried about any repercussions from my family. They had backed off weirdly and oddly and I had ramped up within.

I was colder, number and more relentless in my pursuit to not care about what others said or thought and to not feel. I had surrendered to the idea that I would always disappoint people. I already felt past caring if I was a disappointment, and at a place of not giving an F, within.

I was downplaying what was breaking me. Outwardly I allowed others to see another version of me, one that made it easier to live and less likely for me to have to talk about it. I was tired of trying to explain, of not being heard or asked, so every time I even thought to express myself, it felt like more work than it was to just keep holding it in.

And it worked. People didn't ask. Some avoided the questions because I looked like I might punch someone for questioning anything. And some because they bought it. I actually convinced a long line of therapists, psychologists and others that I was just fine.

Well, this was deep within. I don't give an F was deep on the insides. I didn't just appear not to care. I didn't care. And I was losing hope of ever caring. That's when things got serious.

This weekend I laughed with my friends, my people, for the last time in a really long time. It was our last hurrah without even knowing it. It felt different, but I couldn't pinpoint why, nor did I want to feel any feeling long enough to figure out why or what they might be hinting at. I straight up didn't want to know.

The Family Therapist

I was in my room. This was where I spent a lot of time, as I was grounded most of the time. And when I wasn't, I felt no desire to be downstairs where interactions would drain my soul and make me more irritable and angry and territorial than if I just stayed alone, in my room, minding my own business.

This way, I avoided the fight.

But that night, my father barged in. He always barged in, no knocking. "I own the door" was all he said when I asked him not to.

It was odd. I knew something was off, that this was way more than a casual visit from my dad. We didn't do casual visits. So, this was extra weird.

He started right in. "We're all going together to see this well-known therapist who can help fix this family and you," he said.

I just looked at him.

"Yeah, she never has spots open and she does now, so we are all going together to work this mess out," he added. "Now."

I didn't like it, and I wasn't buying it.

This was my domain, my room to hate him in private, and I felt like I was suffocating with him in there. We never shared this much space anymore. We hated each other and all I wanted to do was to scream, tell him how much I despised him and then disappear. Being in my room with my dad felt like being cornered on a battlefield, and this was normally where I geared and armored up to deal with him.

"There's no way I'm going anywhere with you!" I yelled, and then I started crying—heavy, fierce tears, roaring tears, the type of crying where my body was screaming but it was hard to breathe.

"You have no choice!" he yelled back. "This is what you have to do. This is not a compromise. It is not a conversation. You are a minor and you are going to do what I say. You can go back to your life when you get back."

This went back and forth for hours. And hours. And hours.

I became so exhausted, not only from these hours, but

from the years of feeling trapped and forced to live a life without being seen or heard. It all collided and began to flow and crash all over me from the depths of my soul to the highest volumes of my screams.

He slammed in and out of the room, occasionally going downstairs to yell at my mother. Then my mother would come in, and then he would come back for what seemed like forever.

I finally crawled into my jam-packed closet and called friends to let them hear this mess over the phone. I just wanted to feel like I didn't have to scream or fight or defend or say "no" another stinking time; I just wanted to be left alone for a moment.

Outside the closet door, I heard threats that the cops would be coming to get me, that they would have the police escort me.

I was ready to take 'em all. I wasn't getting in no damn car and sure as hell wasn't going to any far-away specialized therapist that I knew wouldn't be able to mend a man or a family this broken. And I certainly wasn't going with someone who refused to say he caused this deadness in our family. This corpse of a beautiful life that no longer remains…you couldn't revive it.

It was peaceful crammed in this small space, stuffed with clothes and shoeboxes and other stuff. Cuddled up in there, in the dark, I could shut my eyes and lay my tear-soaked cheeks on my knees as I hugged them tight to my chest and sunk into my exhaustion.

Finally, I couldn't cry or scream or defend myself anymore. I was emotionally, physically and mentally grieving and exhausted. I was tired, deep in my soul. I had been depressed and broken and in this toxicity for far too long. My 17-year-old self had had enough.

I was tired of fighting. I just wanted to breathe and get away from all of this. I knew I had to just surrender to this family therapist, this journey to meet the woman who supposedly was "remarkable for fixing families" even though I knew that what it really meant was to "fix" me.

I finally said that I would go but that I wouldn't ride in a car with him for eight hours. I hated him so much that I couldn't bear the sight of his face for five seconds, so I was most definitely not going to be sitting by his ass.

He was just as glad he wouldn't have to ride in the car with me for that many hours. He went to get a rental car for me and my mom.

I had this off feeling as the trip started.

I put some photos of my friends in the car and began playing the music that just days earlier I had cranked up in my girlfriend's car—smoking and jamming with a great buzz.

This time the same tunes felt solemn.

I wondered if they would really send me away.

For eight hours, I kept my headphones on and gazed out the window, so focused on looking like I was pissed off that I didn't recognize where we were going. When I spoke to my mother, she had short answers or ones that didn't feel fully honest. The locations and placements seemed off and we kept driving and driving with no direct destination.

They Went That Far

Finally, we pulled onto a country road and begin to pass what looked like cabins and offices. I didn't see anyone; the area was quiet and secluded, welcoming yet eerie. It felt as though the scenery itself was up to something, but I had no energy left to care.

We walked up a few stairs and slid a glass door. White blinds clung as the beaded strand that opened and closed them rattled. On the other side of the streaky glass, a blonde woman in her mid-30s rose to greet us. She appeared both able to handle her own and compassionate.

My dad sat farthest from the door, and I sat as far from

him as I could get, ready to lay down the truth about my family.

It began just like every other therapy session. My parents talked about how worried they were about me and how angry I was, spilling long scenarios about my unruly behavior and inability to do anything correctly. Then the therapist asked me how I was, and I said "fine" and "I don't want to talk to you or be here." She looked at me with the usual pity.

And I thought, "Well, maybe they were telling the truth—maybe we really did drive all the way here for her to fix the family and not just me."

But as I was thinking that, the sliding door opened, and two men came in.

My mind began to spin, and my hands started to sweat. Flight or fight mode began to build pressure from my stomach up to my throat, and then the truth came. "So, let me tell you what this really is, Jaydee," the therapist said. "It's a seven-to-12-month residential care facility for troubled teens."

Flight or fight died—and sadness, betrayal and grief took over my entire being as my head fell into my hands.

They. Had. Gotten. Me.

They thought I would fight, run or become aggressive; they didn't know that the depression, sadness, abandonment, betrayal, grief and heartache within me was so much worse than any of that.

The rest of that day was a blur of uncontrollable tears and rageful silence.

We walked to the car where I cranked open the trunk to see my bags pre-packed, with loads of new items—tags still on them—that my mother packed out of guilt. They were things I would never wear but that showed their thought-out process, their mapping and planning—and their ultimate betrayal.

I rode in the same damn car that carried all of my stuff and I had no idea, I thought. What a fool I was.

I wasn't speaking to my dad. I was angrily sobbing, unable

to breathe, and I didn't say goodbye or look at him. My mom was in tears and hurting and I wanted to hug her within my soul and say goodbye. But I couldn't lay down my feelings of betrayal long enough to embrace her one last time. She walked away seeing me angry, hurt and betrayed. I didn't know it would be months before I would see or speak to her again.

I felt incredibly broken, angry and abandoned. To top it off, I had to carry my belongings, the ones I had no idea were in the car, from the trunk to my new group home, the wheels of the suitcase rattling on the bumpy back road.

Every second this suitcase jerked at me, I felt fiercer and deeper feelings—rage, sadness, disbelief as well as complete belief, betrayal and abandonment. I wouldn't have put betrayal past my dad but the fact that my mom had participated hurt me to my core. With each jerk of this suitcase, I felt and imagined my friends not hearing from me, noticing I wasn't coming back to school—or their lives. I never got to say goodbye.

I walked into my new home and faces peered over the top of the stairs; they came out of their rooms and stared at me blankly. More faces were in the living room. I felt like they were all trying to figure out where I had come from, what I was about, why I was sent there, so curious about this white-blonde, orange-tanned angry girl. But I didn't want to know a single one of them.

I was going to get out of this joint.

I was standing in a room with bunk beds and a desk, looking at the trash bags full of my clothing. I couldn't even listen to what the tech helping me was talking about because I was still in such disbelief that my clothing and pillows and hygiene products were all packed and thrown into bags way before I even knew they were thinking about this. I was choking back what felt like years of sadness and tears. I wanted so badly to just be angry, but I felt so so much more.

I began to toss the clothes around, screaming angry profanities and cynical reviews of the clothing chosen for me that I swore I would never wear in my lifetime. Not only was it ugly but it was chosen for me and packed deceitfully, and I wanted nothing to do with any of it. I would rather have walked around for a year in only the clothing I arrived in—a black shirt and jeans and white knock-off Ugg boots, than wear any of it.

And it wasn't because I liked this outfit...it was because I *chose* to wear it. *None of this* I chose for myself.

I wanted so badly to just fight and rock out, to run away through the woods outside of that cabin but I was on such a high level of betrayal that I sat there sobbing uncontrollably. Eventually, the person holding the *Bible of Residential Care Facility Life* read it out loud to me.

I walked around angry and quiet and with a constant "don't F with me" expression.

(I later found out that face was also permanent at home.)

I don't care about you.

You don't care about me.

I don't care about anything.

I'm going to get out of here.

These people are crazy and are smiling here. Do they not know *everyone gave up on them?*

Level One

Welcome to Level One—you have zero personal space or freedom.

No cursing. Five-foot distance from any "big," which is what they called an adult. You had to ask to do pretty much anything: "Can I go up, can I go down, can I go in, can I go out, can I come in, can I get up, can I eat?"

And we weren't allowed to talk to each other without permission. It was intended to prevent troubled teens from concocting conspiracy plans to flee into the woods, get off the grounds or cause any other kind of mischief. Well, good thing for me, I didn't want to speak to anyone anyway.

My mother said she called to check in every day. The director of this jail in the woods was telling her that I was sitting alone, looking angry and not the tiniest bit interested in carrying on a conversation with anyone.

At least he was honest because that was accurate. I was constantly in the state of "pissed."

In the program, there were four levels, and I was focused on the fourth—to get out.

With each level came new responsibilities, more goals to achieve and more personal growth that mirrored your commitment to growing and thriving and being prepared to enter back into your previous reality with a new-found mindset and sense of commitment to who you strive to be.

Resiliency Factors

I am often asked what I gained from that time or if it was really beneficial. For many years I said no, it didn't really benefit my life, and without hesitation, I would still say that it didn't help and was a bit traumatizing to be sent away so abruptly.

Even if I was reckless, even if I was doing reckless things, even if I was unhappy and making mistake after mistake and digging myself into a deeper and bigger hole of confusion and sadness and depression, I was still completely uprooted without any knowledge that my life was about to take a huge shift.

Seven-and-a-half months is a long time, and each day and hour was accounted for in my life journey. I remember the countless minutes that felt like months and the moments that felt like days that I journaled through, that I ran through, that I cried through and screamed through. I persevered through to be able to say I was a graduate of a program that I never signed up for and had never planned to enter.

I didn't realize that I found a lot of resiliency factors during those seven-and-a-half months.

Resiliency factors are people, environments, spaces, songs, books, connections, relationships, sources of recovery, sobriety —whatever gives you just enough light to trudge a few more steps in your trenches with a desire to one day fully thrive and be who you are supposed to be.

Here I began to see the beauty, the art and the gift of questioning.

I have a deep belief that questioning and intimacy in connection can change our relationships in a dramatic way.

When we take intentional time to inquire, engage and be still in communication—a non-romantic intimacy is created.

Intentional reciprocal communication. Can. change. This. world.

Here, I hesitate; I linger.

For some reason, this chapter of my life does not light my fire but gives me lots of mixed feels.

What I took and gained from that experience had little to do with the reasons I was sent there to begin with.

Sometimes we live in rebellion and anger that's covering some other deep feels. I had so many feels underneath—lying dormant, hidden and masked—I couldn't really tell what was there anymore.

I was sent because I was rebellious.

I was sent because I had anger issues, because no one knew how to handle me any longer.

I was sent because I was failing academically.

I was sent because my father said I was "ruining our family," and I couldn't be told "no."

I was sent because I didn't know how to speak in tones that weren't glass shattering and because I couldn't get along with my father.

I was sent because I didn't fit the mold my father wanted me to.

I was sent because I was done pretending that "all was good," that my family was good, that I was good.

I was sent because I was done trying to fit the mold of a good, well-mannered, Jesus-loving private-schooled little girl, with no voice and no opinion, who was okay that life within my home was turmoil.

I was sent because I took off that mask and chose to just *be* and with that came *truth*—reckless and messy, authentic and loud truth in every facet of my life.

But I was really there because I had lost hope and stopped dreaming.

I was there because I was so constantly disappointed— disappointed that my dad was not sober, disappointed that I wasn't heard or seen or asked, disappointed that people judged me or disciplined me instead of listening to me or seeing what may be wrong.

I was there because I gave up on being asked or seen and didn't care what judgments I felt were cast on me as well as spoken to me and behind my back. No one knew me and I was always seen as the kid who made mistakes.

I was there because I didn't care how I was even seen.

I was there because I both wanted to disappear and desperately needed to be seen at the same time.

I was there because I had a voice, an opinion other than what was expected of me.

I was there because I wasn't squishing and morphing myself into the too-small box they determined I belonged in.

Because of the real reasons I was there, I still benefit from what I took away. Whether that was what was written on my admissions paperwork or not, it was what I was destined to learn to become the woman I am today, and I honor that instead of being ashamed that I wasn't a completely perfect and transformed human when I went home.

Being Seen

For a very long time I tried to "fake it to get out." I tried to, each session, pretend I was fine, all was dandy, and I was "fixed" after a few short weeks. Then, one day, I realized I wasn't going anywhere; my parents had left and were not coming back. I was here for the long haul.

That day I slammed the sliding glass door and took my seat fiercely as the therapist audaciously asked, "How are you?"

How Am I?

"Oh, all right," I said. "The 400 times you've asked before, I've lied. So today, since I'm not getting the get-out-of-jail-free card, I'll let you have it."

I screamed and cried and let out all the cuss words I had harbored in my head since I'd sat in that exact seat for the first time.

"I fucking hate it! I fucking hate all of it! I was stripped from everything I knew—I was punished and it completely ruined my life!" I yelled. "I am *just angry* because my family and life suck. I'm pissed my dad went home and I'm the one who was sent away and I fucking hate him so much. I'm mad he blames me when he caused me to become this angry and resentful and cold."

More F more F more F thattttttttt. Tears came from places within I didn't even know existed anymore and I felt this huge relief of pain and anger escaping from my trapped lungs as I felt truth. I thought for sure that now she was never going to let me leave, that I was about to have some kind of punishment. She's going to try to find me 50 meds, I thought. I'm about to be deemed *aggressive*.

I didn't look up because I knew what I'd shrieked was unacceptable.

Instead, she rocked my world and simply said, "Jaydee, welcome. Now you can do the work you need to do."

I will remember the moment of being seen in all my feelings that day for the rest of my life.

She didn't scold me, tell me not to be so angry, tell me to tone down my voice or watch my language. She didn't grab me a tissue or tell me I was never going to get past Level One.

She said "hey" to me all over again, welcoming all my hurt and pain and truth.

She let me know it was okay to feel boldly and bravely and be seen at the same time.

To be seen in the midst of healing is one of the most radical things we can do for another. That right there changed my view of life.

She was right; I never showed up without my feels or without my truth ever again in her presence. She had welcomed me, and I was never going to relinquish my ability to be me in that space ever again.

Thank you for seeing me.

Remembering

When we took my first photo of our room, I asked them to take the shot over and over again because I didn't like my smile. I didn't remember how to smile. It was around Christmas and we had Christmas T-shirts on that we had created for a "room night." I still barely knew those people, yet now I was living bunk to bunk with them and taking photos with them. I wasn't used to taking photos and I didn't think I would want to remember this time.

I looked so not happy and my smile was forced, so I asked to try and try again. I just couldn't get this smiling thing right, but for once I realized that something about myself didn't feel right and I wanted to work on it. I wanted to try to smile over and over again, but I knew somewhere deep inside of me this was a soul thing, not a digital camera thing.

As part of my program, I volunteered at a teen mom

center, watching their babies so they could access resources and fill a trash bag full of donated baby items. I had to write my story and present a piece of it to my home. And something about the teen mom center moved me so much that, for the first time, I cried in front of the girls I lived with. One of them said to me after, "Whoa, you cry? I wasn't sure you felt anything but anger."

I opened up, after time—connecting with girls who became my family, and, if they had attempted suicide, telling them they couldn't go, I didn't want them to. So many girls dropped their bags at the same door I did, and after I'd been there a while, I could see all of them. I looked forward to sliding that same glass door back and trudging through my trenches with my therapist.

Every weekend we had a "room night" and a "house night." One night we did an activity with our roommates— with two littles and a big—like going to a coffee shop. And on "house nights" we did something with the entire girls' house— some activity, a themed night or an outing to an event in the city or to a coffee shop with board games where we could use our allowances to buy steamed milk or hot chocolate. I loved getting to put on makeup and wearing something different. On those nights, I took long showers and felt like I was a normal human being, going and doing something. I so wanted connection, normality, and to live a normal life again.

I loved the smell of coffee shops and began to love the experience of visiting so many different ones, but I hadn't found my love for coffee yet, so I got "vanilla creamers" with my allowance money. My only other treat was peanut butter Ritz crackers I got on our random gas station trips.

I cried when I got letters from home, frustrated that my friends were getting closer while I was becoming a faint memory, realizing their lives were going on without me. I couldn't wait for my phone call time and to be able to hear my mom's voice as I literally tried to breathe it in. I saw everyone's hard days. I saw their tears, their discoveries, their hard phone calls, their "I didn't level up" and their faces as they walked back into the house after hard and heavy therapy sessions.

We took long treks, in all weather, to the church way down the road that we were forced to attend. I refused to raise my hands or sing during worship. I didn't feel judged for that and actually felt damn good about taking ownership and acknowledging that me and God were in a quarrel and He knew I just wasn't singing to him right then and that was okay. I cleaned cars and vacuumed and sprayed the pews of that church. And in each place, we shared life, shared our truths—our hatred for those who had hurt us and our anger for what got us here.

I had short phone calls with my mom, tucked into a quiet spot in the midst of my house's turmoil. I wanted to hear my mom's voice even if it was for only 10 minutes. She felt like home. I cried or screamed through our calls, sometimes bursting with betrayal and rage. I walked through my healing and then backtracked if I felt I had revealed something that was "too much," something which might make her feel she should keep me there longer. I felt a fierce conflict between sharing truth and being present while also desperately wanting to leave and feeling like I needed to pretend I was "fixed" so I could. I hoped and sometimes thought when I begged to go home that my mom would cave and come get me, but she didn't.

My dad would pop in the phone calls, making me so angry that I would hang up. I eventually stopped speaking with my mom, since getting to hear her voice meant also hearing his.

We got so excited when people left for their weekends and not for one moment did we steal their joy to think of ourselves. We gathered around our people when they had to come back to us—hearing about their lives, their grief and pain, and the joy they had while being home. We heard if they snuck a smoke in or if they snuck a night in with their crush.

Home visits were times we could feel real, embrace our people, our friends and our "normal" lives. But, in each moment we knew we'd have to head back to the life we'd been forced to live—residential care life. It was hard to fully embrace the joy of being home knowing we'd have to go back. When we arrived back, we handed our bags over to be searched and sunk back into group home life, sometimes with a fierce "I'm going to get out of here and get back home vibe" and sometimes with a steady slope of sadness that was really hard to detach from.

Forgiveness

I used to never read.

I spent many of my childhood years on a bean bag sprawled amidst children's books in my parents' bookstores with no desire to crack one of them open.

Even in high school, I skimmed.

I scanned for specific words to find whatever answer I needed.

Or I snagged the movie of the book to do a school project, if I did the project at all. My mom was tired of fighting me, so she supported the trips to Blockbuster.

The first book I genuinely connected with on any level was *The Art of Forgiving* by Lewis B. Smedes. This book was given to me by the therapist at my residential care facility.

Of course, I wasn't going to blow off an assignment that would help me get to the next level of the program, a next step to *getting out* of the program. But she also had me journaling with it; it's like she knew I was going to try to skim it or something.

That book was the beginning of what I would call my soul grind.

I got sucked in, had my first awe moments, wanted to read it and connected with this book in a way that made sense. I began to resonate with it, gain enlightenment from it and feel weights lifted by its wisdom.

This book completely rocked my view and battle with forgiveness.

I had it all wrong.

I saw forgiveness as utter weakness.

I defined it mentally and emotionally as "you win, and I lose."

I had to hold tight to the rage, bitterness and wrongness of my father's addiction because if I let him know I forgave him, let him know I was choosing to forgive myself for becoming so enraged because of him, or allowed him to see how the struggle within me was so much because of him, he would win. He would feel like I swept all his destructive decisions away, that I was cool with them. Or I felt he would think I was going to just let many years of watching him fall into toxicity and addiction be just a thing of the past.

It was my childhood.

It was what made me rage-filled and unable to spend nights over with my friends because I feared for my mom.

It was me feeling guilty for choosing who to ride home with—my mom or dad.

It was the hurt and anger I carried from when I saw him look a woman up and down or prioritized her while criticizing my mom.

It was always having her on my mind and, while I was home, always having an ear to the door.

It was needing my voice to ignite or awaken hers.

It was arguing and fighting him.

It was seeing her in her sadness, silence and submission.

It was the deep sorrow and sadness and protection I felt for her always.

It was my sadness and my inability to connect with my father.

It was not having conversations with him.

It was screaming and spending hours in my room grounded and misunderstood.

It was my inability to be good enough.

It was my lack of self-worth.

It was me in my scrubs at Our Lady of Peace mental institution because I was deemed suicidal.

It was alcohol and cigarettes.

It was not being able to ask for help in school because I knew I wouldn't meet his standards.

It was the grief of a father I vaguely remembered being my hero when I was a little girl.

It was me dying my hair so many colors and still not feeling like I knew who I was.

It was wanting the "you did so awesome" after my games or meets and instead always hearing what I did wrong.

It was seeing my sisters hurt and hustle for their worth from him and not be celebrated for how amazing they were.

Forgiveness was so big for me; it felt like all of me, every aspect of me, was touched by the question of forgiveness.

It felt like I was saying so many years that ruined my life were justified.

Forgiving him felt like it was saying all that was okay.

And my stubborn and fiercely loving self refused to allow him to have that.

I wasn't letting him win.

I wasn't backing down.

I wasn't going to allow him to see pain or sadness or grief.

I wasn't going to be the weak one when I knew I was the only one battling him.

But what I was doing by not forgiving him, by not forgiving myself, was becoming him.

So, I drifted into pills, unhealthy relationships, drugs, alcohol, seeking validation from boys and men who didn't care, into the inability to see my worth or ignite my passions and pursue my dreams. It made me very, very hard-hearted. It made me choose numbing instead of feeling.

He wasn't winning but I sure wasn't either.

I was dying inside, which could've made me die all over.

If that therapist hadn't so beautifully forced me to read this book, I would still be holding on to many, many, many things that did not serve me.

The book made me breathe and finally stop carrying so much hatred and rage. Instead I could choose to love myself and honor every stinking piece of it. I could choose to let go of some parts, work through others, grow, forgive and seek wisdom, guidance, boundaries and my truth through it all.

And the best part: it was no one's business that I was working on forgiveness.

It was mine.

A sacred move of my soul.

Back to the Steps

I walked into that residential home with zero independence, no freedom to talk to others and no permission to legit ever be by myself except to pee. I had to stay at a five-foot distance from a "Big," which is what they called counselors and other adults, and to top it off we had to have a certain amount of protein at dinner, do chores and attend school with no communication with others—and, at Level One, no communication with my world at home.

Each level brought greater responsibility, fewer restrictions, more goals and opportunities to accomplish and increased access to my at-home community—trips home for short visits—and, after many months, opportunities to mingle for very short periods with the boys at the home across the way (ooh la la). Eventually, it even meant email access. Of course, email was previewed and read and able to be seen by my therapist—aka no privacy, but that was my own family's doing. They made the list of who I could contact and how private these conversations could be. They didn't trust me, so they said all my mail had to be reviewed by my therapist.

Level One was *rough*. But to be honest, the last level was just as hard as the first. I don't know what it is about being almost done with something, but when I was *this* close to finishing, I was jumping out of my skin and ready to roll. I thought every day felt like a year and the momentum and drive I needed to get through some of the toughest times of my life was tapping out, mind on E, no gas left in this tank.

Everyone had their trenches, that's for sure.

Our home had a cabin feel with wooden panels, carpet bunk beds and rooms shared with complete strangers—until we chose to actually get to know one another.

I had to relearn what it was like to speak respectfully to another human. I had to learn how to smile again, how to breathe and be still, how to take in life and not despise it.

I had to figure out what honesty felt like, and how to express myself other than in razor blades to my wrist and thighs, and screaming at the top of my lungs—or in a car or parking lot as my face went numb from drinking too much Heaven Hill from a water bottle.

Level Four

My Big at the facility made the shape of "Level Four" on the ground out of graham crackers for me to see after I left one of my sessions. I remember looking at the number four like I never had before. *I had made it to the end.*

This was the end I had wanted since I stepped in.

I remembered when they made me VP of the home. And then the president.

I also remembered planning an in-house prom so that we could feel, for once, like we weren't missing out on something.

I remembered turning 18—and knowing I could walk, could finally leave.

I remembered knowing that I didn't go all this way to not graduate this damn place.

The women who trudged this time with me relentlessly day in and day out stood in front of a mic at my graduation and talked about me in the most beautiful way I had ever heard, in a way that was in no way, shape or form surface level. They loved me past my intake and all up in my journey and with my calloused and cold and rough-edged ways. I was going to miss some of these crazy people. I knew no one at home would ever truly understand what that was like.

I still hated my dad. Some of those feelings were gone but the ones that remained I understood more honestly. They felt validated and honored.

I walked that pavement for the last time and hugged these epic humans who had tear-filled eyes, and I dropped hand-written notes on the bunk bed of everyone who loved me up.

I wasn't going to miss this place, but I was going to miss some of them.

I began to realize, I loved still, I cared still. And I now felt in a different way than I had when I walked in.

Love Languages

I have read and taken the quizzes to try to learn how I best love others and how I'm best loved. These tools help us understand how we are wired, how we give love and how we receive it. They help you open the door to those you love to guide these conversations so that both parties can see the differences. There are ways I have discovered I feel loved, which includes coffee and soulful conversations: I feel loved and like I can best give love over coffee and in deep diving into my peoples' souls in conversation. This is where love is sourced for me.

The Gift of Questioning—questioning and the ability to

be asked questions—is a love language, a gateway and an access to someone's soul.

It takes both asking the question and actively providing space for the other to be seen and heard and sat with while the question is answered.

I mean, how many times have you been asked, "Hey, how are you doing?" and, as you go to give an answer, the person is already halfway down the hallway with their back to you, mid wave?

You ask, you provide space and you connect with this beautiful human that is allowing you to see them in their response.

That right there is what I am talking about.

It's about more than how you are. It's about specific, non-surface questions.

It's about where do you come from and where do you plan on going.

It's who you truly are and what are you made of.

In the simplest of forms, instead of just "Hey," it's "How was your weekend, tell me about it," as a person hurries into work on a Monday morning and sits next to you before they grind through massive amounts of emails, trying to earn some "out of the office" life.

The gift of questioning opens an opportunity for connection and intimacy. When you ignite someone's soul and vice versa, a deep connection is made, where both parties feel seen. And we all yearn to be seen and to have someone ask authentically about who we are and hold tight long enough to hear us in it.

When we ask and sit, we learn.

When we ask and sit, we connect.

When we dig into our trenches together and talk about our ups and downs, we connect.

How will you heal if you don't ask yourself pivotal questions?

How will you truly connect if you don't ask soul-digging questions?

You won't.

And there were too few coffees, soul-deep convos and questions in my future as I headed home.

7

Same Stuff, 7½ Months Later

I left, but nothing had changed.

I came home and was treated the same.

I arrived home in June. The next time I touched alcohol to my lips was July 4th.

That was definitely not in the contract between my parents and me that I signed prior to graduating and leaving the program.

But I wanted to do it all.

This time, there was more judgment as people glared when I lifted alcohol to my lips. I knew they saw me as someone who hadn't changed—"still a rebel" and "still no good."

Senior year was rough. Trying to fit into a former mold was really difficult. Friendships faded, others evolved, talks began to change, girls were becoming women and virgins becoming "whores." Sitting in the back of class, in math, which I never paid attention to, I was sharing stories of experimentation in a realm our private Christian school would have sent us to the gates of Hades for. My parents, peers and uh anyone in the huge but tiny city already had their assumptions about me.

But the truth was that I was still a virgin. No guy had actually gotten what everyone thought I was giving out freely to any guy who caught up with me on a Sonic-slush-and-Heaven-Hill, face-go-numb night. Well, this was the year the liquor and the beer and the pills and the parties and the pure rebellion went full throttle.

It felt like I was reliving the same nightmare.

The anger was beginning to rustle up and let me know it had only been dormant. The bitterness began to rise up and the trapped in my own life rebellion began to feel known and heard and necessary again.

All of this, all too familiar. All of this had already exhausted me, and I knew it was all going to bring some radical rattling to my soul.

I felt even more judged and rebellious in my rebellion. People knew I had disappeared. They knew I had come back. They were expecting me to be fixed, healed, changed and now when I hit a high or drank a beer, they knew I hadn't. There was more that I needed to numb out, more I had to shake off and this time, more of a drive and need to do it. And I did, more and worse.

One night, I read an email on the computer I used from time to time in my sister's old room. It was to my therapist at the residential care facility, from my parents, pleading and asking why I had not changed, why I was still a mess, why I was not all healed and all dandy. It sounded like they had made a very large purchase and wanted their money back in full after signing a contract where there were no refunds—something I found out when I saw many, many envelopes with Shelterwood written on them. They were paying for that place for a very long time.

The first evening I slipped the white, round antidote in my mouth recreationally, it was given to me by a soul who was always with me in my trenches, not in a "I want you to feign this, and need this to live, and seep into addiction" way, but in an "I'm going to allow you to have this because I know you're in pain, don't take this and that together, but just do one" caring way. He gave it to me and watched out for me, not wanting me to do too much or drift away into numbness. I wanted to both drink and take it and he told me I couldn't do both. In a messed-up way, it was almost like he cared enough to help numb my pain. He wanted to slip into the silence of highs amongst chaos with me, and just let us be still in the fog.

He slipped it into my hand and my love for this secretive type of high began. It was perfect. It didn't have a scent. It wasn't caught on a breathalyzer and I could hang with all the private God-loving kids and not think about being judged and feeling like I could never truly be myself.

I would rather be with them high. I wanted to be numb on the inside but not be shamed, shunned, punished on the outside. This was the cure to my inability to be heard. It made sense. And I began to crave this silent healer. It wasn't hard to get, nor was I judged for having it. We would sit in his garage surrounded by others getting high in various ways, as my friend played the piano, so his playing raised my every goose-bump and made my whole high body fall in love with its rhythm. The lights were chilled, the joint was passed, the pills traded and we all crept into a smoke-infused, mellow zone.

Some of the days we showed up to rage—well, I would rage too hard and pass out, crash into something or have that one senior crush fight someone over a camera I said they lost when really I had no idea where it was because I was such a drunken mess. A state of oblivion.

Everyone there had epic gifts, talents, dreams and no one was pursuing them, no one channeling their full potential, no one asking more of each other or telling them they could do more, be more, take their epic magic and spread it to everyone.

We showed up, we smoked up and we carried on.

There was also something about this space where there

was no judgment. The person I sat next to as he played made me feel safe in my intoxication, and I could chain smoke all day and then get offered some of his. It was, for me, a rare sense of community, inclusion and belonging—for a life of not fully living as I held onto something, a white sphered something or several liquid somethings that sugarcoated and numbed the process of grinding, trying, loving and living.

Plan B

Our school had a "put your questions on this card and fold it and stick it in this box and the nurse will "probably not answer it" type of sex ed, the type where you don't want to ask because you know the answer is "Don't do it." Everyone in the class looked around sheepishly, knowing that not one of us was asking a question, especially in a bright color ink that was clearly legible and identified the asker and suggested that we were the only ones that wanted to know what sex was. We knew that then we would be judged for wondering or daring to go there.

The first time I had sex, I hated it. I honestly had no hope or knowledge of what it would feel like, look like or be like and because of that, I didn't have high expectations. But I sure didn't think it would go down that way. I thought first times were supposed to be epic, fireworks and a story you would tell people down the road about your first-time lovemaking sesh with your first-ever love. Yeah, not so much.

I got rug burn from being in a house that was under renovations—our stomping grounds for a dance after-party. I wasn't dating him, for real didn't like him and he was a last-minute date option. He got with one of my friends soon after.

The next morning started the Plan B saga of my life, as well as a series of sexual experiences with other boys and thoughts along the lines of "I mean nothing," "I guess I'll just drink since I know what's coming," "This is what he wants,"

"It'll be over soon," "Maybe now he'll like me" and "Just give it up, it's just my body" decline of my self-worth. It was what kept me from knowing my epic worth.

At this point, I was drinking and trying to keep up, with life, with the accomplishments and the steps of the girls around me—with our status, my rebellion and my coldness.

Once I slipped into the realm of not respecting self, not realizing my own worth, and being so stuck in the trenches of sadness, questioning, grief and rebellion, I was in a dangerous and very low place.

I was getting ready for one night at a friend's. Who knows what lie I told my parents in order to free myself from the grip of being forever in trouble. But I do remember trying to explain it the next day, after chugging what was left of my vodka on the way home because I knew I was so very grounded for life. I figured I might as well go out with a banger.

"I mean which do I start with—where I spent the night or that I just got out of handcuffs? Hmm.

Yeah, I'll drink the rest of this real quick."

The night before I had gone to a college baseball game. I was there to be a part of fixing up a girl I wasn't very close with and a ballplayer. The next thing I knew I was at my friend's boyfriend's home playing beer pong. I remember my exact moment of acceptance, the exact moment when I realized the people in the room had begun to pair off and the guy playing pong by me was the one I was slotted for.

Unworthy

I lifted a beer to my mouth and had another shot. I accepted I was going to stay at the house of someone I had just met, lay in his bed and have sex with a guy I didn't even know. This was the night life, this was the life I signed up for that accompanied partying and being the one that sleeps over and gets hit up by boys after late nights and drunken parties, the drunken senior girl who had sex with the university baseball player.

I was lucky right? Yeah…no.

I began drinking to ensure the next few hours and next morning would be faint, unclear and not carry many feels. I already knew where this was all going.

I spent the night laying in a stranger's bed after once again giving my body away and was still feeling very drunk as I walked into my friend's home the next morning in the previous night's clothes. My friends laughed and asked how it was and we joked about it. I began to change, standing in the living room staring at my phone and wondering if I would ever hear from this dude again and, in the same instant, shrugging it off, trying to feel as though I should "play it cool" and not care—I mean, this is what people do, right? This is when I began the loop of feeling off, giving my body away being seen in this way. It rattled me but I thought, "Don't give an F, Jaydee, it'll only hurt you in the long haul if you do."

Normally I Plan B'd it, took the Plan B pill and then carried on with life, getting nothing in return. My thinking towards any boy that I liked was "I'm yours" and "I owe you this." This also created a dynamic that I was to perform, give and do the walk of shame the morning after—feeling used and partially mastering a craft that wasn't appreciated, valued or even reciprocated.

Drink, give, walk away, repeat. The mornings after eventually didn't include wondering if he would call because I just would carry on. I stopped considering the possibility that there would be a "Nice seeing you" or "Can I take you out?" or "Let's get dinner" because I knew I was only sought and wanted for one thing.

Breathalyzer

The next morning, my friend, a couple of guys and I were in a badass sports car going 90 miles an hour on winding back roads. You know that feeling you get when you know things could go wrong—that rattled rising up in your chest? You either speak to it or shut it down and change it to the thought "Everything will be just fine, chill."

This whole car ride, I was exchanging liquor for my feelings, hoping it would just coat over them so I couldn't let my fear and shame rise enough to make me a buzz-killing party pooper. I didn't want to be the buzz-killer that day, or any day.

I went from one lie straight to the next.

I couldn't live this life and tell the truth.

I couldn't live this life and be honest with myself, my parents, with anyone.

I didn't know what to feel or even what felt right or wrong any more.

We were driving to the lake in our two-piece bathing suits. I didn't like my bod in a bathing suit and I felt out of place and drunkenly guilty and small from the night before, but I was trying to feel powerful in a woman-hear-me-roar type of way on our next adventure, which was to go boating and bring all the liquor with us.

Underage – check.

Not enough life jackets on board – check.

Not able to drive a boat – check.

Not legal to have alcohol in our underage possession-check.

Drinking while driving a boat anyway – check.

It was a great setup.

At first, it was the time of our lives: selfies, cranked-up music, jumping off and back on the boat.

Shots, shots, shots, beer, beer, beer.

Living the legit life.

Did you know there are boats that have police lights?

Yup. The lights ramped up and the next thing we knew, the party was over.

We were drunkenly trying to hide the liquor and dump some of the booze in the lake and hold tight to the tiny bit of sobriety we could muster.

I had no idea how breathalyzers worked so I figured if I blew as hard as I could, it would show that I was able to do so, which would show that for sure, wasn't intoxicated—that I was fully capable of breathing the hardest of the crew. Turns out I actually registered as the most intoxicated since I was blowing alcohol into the device as hard as I could.

The next thing I knew, I was handcuffed and wailing, telling the cops they were ruining my life, with my arms twisted up behind my back.

We were taken to a holding station where I made my calls and finally got bail money from one of the really good friends who had otherwise given up on me. She was one of the people I wrote to from my residential care facility, but we'd had a falling out because of my drinking and nonsense and drama. She didn't talk much after picking me up—I said thank you and gave her 20 bucks for bail. Then I got a ride to my car, and drove to a huge Walmart near home, where I sat in the parking lot and called my dad to tell him about the arrest before finishing up the leftover vodka and heading home.

I knew my already no-life was over.

He always told me to not call him if I got locked up because he would leave me there, so I knew this one would not go well.

That slightly tipsy drive back home was one I wanted to both last forever and speed up so I could get the "You are a failure at life" speech over.

It was kinda like the moments I got in trouble at school when I was younger and forced my mom to spank me first so my dad couldn't when he got home after work later that day. I also always wore five layers when having this convo with my mom. I was golden at not getting whooped hard.

Thankful for the buzz I still had, I opened the door and found I had an audience. Sat myself down and for the first time in my life, heard my mom yell. She was so angry and frustrated that she couldn't breathe; her face even turned a shade of red as she paced in front of me. My dad was pissed, but this was nothing new. I was so shocked about my mom that he was just white noise.

Then she asked, *"Are you still drunk?"* And at that point I knew it was my cue to sway my numbed self up the stairs.

Well, that was a weekend for the shame books.

I cleaned cop cars for nine hours straight because of this day and stood in front of a judge and told her I was flat out guilty, while all my friend's attorneys stood there for them.

I was to "learn my lesson."

As the man at the shop told me while I was doing my community service hours, "You can drink—just don't do it on a boat, geez."

Noted.

Finishing Up

Walking down the halls that next Monday at school, I knew that some people knew about my arrest. If the word spread any further, I wouldn't be graduating. The girl went to my school and the two boys did not. People were likely to find out and my Christian school didn't look highly on its students getting handcuffed over the weekend. And I was already not well thought of at that point.

I was losing some friendships because of drinking.

They knew I was back in the muck of my life and wading deeper.

And honestly, I told them that in numbness I felt better, that I liked life better this way.

But I didn't stop.

I was drinking, day drinking, drinking and driving.

I went to events in some form of high and pills were now my preferred go-to.

My mom and I had already bought a prom dress—my mom's last attempt to make it so that I could attend (as far as my dad was concerned, I was grounded for the rest of my life).

Pretty sure my mom felt some fierce guilt for the fact that I missed my junior prom since they'd sent me away, so I was taking what I could get.

I snagged a random date and showed up for the pics and had an exact time I needed to be home.

No after-parties for this one, just a quick drive through Taco Bell.

Now even those I loved were beginning to see I was lost, and I didn't care how lost I was.

I had many families and friends that took me in and loved me up, stayed with me through the times but I had one ride or die...that never, no matter what, ever left my side.

She rocked short brown hair, despised skirts and anything girly, she rocked her own style and a laugh that would have everyone rolling right along with her. She was chill and down to do whatever, she didn't let everyone in, and I felt sacred to be one of those few. She had her tough side but to her friends she was hilarious and full of compassion and loyalty and massive amounts of love. She was my go-to when life was rough, my pal for long car rides when we needed them, my pull up to her parents curb pal who would come outside and hear me roar, my safety, my second call, my best friend. I don't think I could've made it through high school without her.

I think of her and her family often. People like that leave an imprint on your soul and a mark on your own personal grind when they are in your trenches with you. Still, for some, enough is enough. It gets too hard.

And that time was now for most of them.

Glad You Made It

At certain times, I never thought I would graduate, nor did I care. All I wanted now was freedom. I was the first to turn 16 in my high school and one of the last to actually be able to get my license and drive. I drove the hand-me-down car which both my sisters had driven before. It had Mardi Gras beads hanging off the rearview mirror and I sent up a prayer every day—one with some curse words involved—in the hope that my car would actually rev up when school was over for the day. I did love this gold car, though, even on the days I could barely get it to roll out of the senior lot, bumping along and thrumming from the mixed CDs I rocked to at an extremely loud volume. I took out my Camel Light pink packs, hidden in my console, to chain smoke on the back-winding roads home.

And then I finally somehow graduated. I was handed my diploma and escorted down the stairs of the stage as our vice principal said, "Jaydee, I'm so glad you made it." Psh, you and me both.

8

College Visits

I had visited many universities; well, partied at many of them. I fell in love with a university an hour-and-a-half away from home. I loved the feel of the campus and the community feel. It was right up my alley—the parties seemed to be always alive and wild and infused with college feels...free, social, carefree, independent. I could see myself living there, walking the campus, and I felt the energy and desire to be free and experience life uncensored and unapologetically. No boundaries.

All of these visits were a waste—my parents were never going to allow my raging extrovert self to go to a school that screamed of reckless and fun. But my mind was made up.

Bad Idea

The only school my parents would allow me to go was the Baptist college in Pennsylvania where my dad worked at the time, so we were able to get a deal on tuition. I was angry and annoyed when I was dropped off to do freshman orientation at this cult-like school. My dad said, "College isn't for all, but you're going to give it a try."

It was a place where shoulders couldn't be revealed, pants

couldn't be too tight, skirts couldn't be too short, where hand-holding was correlated with sex and genders were divided by separate sidewalks, just in case you felt tempted to look at someone in a risky you-may-get-prego-by-looking type of way.

My last attempts at a relationship with my dad were unraveling. We had struggled for years and it was not getting better; distance was the only way we could function. We were blood, but barely even tolerated the other's name being mentioned. Even with all this pain, there were days I wanted a father, a man's perspective, a tough bit of love and protection.

I would seek a smile, an approval, a "good job" or an "I'm proud of you." I would pretend to want nothing to do with him yet would walk by him after chapel to try to get a goofy hello or grab my salad while he also took a break in the cafeteria and stop by his table to say a few words. I hated him so badly but also deeply wanted some type of affirmation—a claiming that I in fact was his daughter. But I never could get that.

Every time, I was let down in my hopes he would fill the void and erase the pain of not having a father. With each disappointment, I went further back into resentment and pain. I would bring hope but walk away with more pain and additional shame for even wanting something so unattainable to begin with. I tried so hard to lay to rest the shame I felt about wanting a relationship with him, about wanting to be seen and heard and asked. I would wipe out the past and try again and again to see if it would be different. It never was. And I became harder and colder with each let-down.

Cigarettes

I had just gotten to the university when I found a stump near the woods where I could secretively smoke a cigarette and call my boyfriend back home to cry about how badly I felt and how pissed I was to be stuck again in a place where I didn't belong. I wrapped up the call to head into Freshman Meet and Greet, coating myself in Bath and Body Work Spray, and put five pieces of gum in my mouth to kill the stench of smoke. Then I entered a gym full of people who would never dare smoke a cigarette, who if they smelled it on me—and my too tight shirt and bright purple pants—would deem me "sinful."

I stuck out like a dragster in a parking lot full of Buicks. I didn't know if it was because of my "don't mess with me" face or the fact that I just rolled my eyes at students and teachers who tried to connect with me during freshman orientation. Maybe both.

It felt like the private school and all the vacation Bible school weeks and summer Jesus camps I was forced to attend as a kid—weekly chapels and weekly Bible courses. At the private school, my parents and I had had to sign a contract that we would attend a church consistently and remain members. The contract also said I would not drink. Since my dad was in seminary at that time, we also had to sign a contract to solely attend Baptist church while he worked there and went to school there. Every Sunday morning, Sunday evening and Wednesday night. I went for the social gatherings but even that felt uneasy, like a chore. The feeling of trying to fit constantly into molds and places where I never truly felt I belonged, no matter how much I changed my clothes, was always uncomfortable.

And then, in college, when I was officially grown, there I was, still being forced to attend school like I was 13. I would peer over the rows as I saw my dad at the mandatory chapels, singing along at worship as I wondered who that human was and if anyone knew that he had left, run away from his family —that he had an addiction, didn't have a relationship with us and was singing to a God I didn't want to claim as mine.

I hiked up the nearby mountains, with my purse full of perfume and mints, sugar coating my daily reality, breathing in the cold air, catching a quick breath of nicotine to soften the blow of my depression, and trucking back down the hill to once again try to be someone that fit into this new box made for me.

Benadryl and Tylenol PM were my savior Friday evenings; I could knock out and sleep through the majority of the next day—the only day my room wasn't checked, the only day I didn't have an alarm buzzing in my ear telling me to wake up and once again try to morph myself into versions of myself I didn't want to be. I could sleep and recklessly wake up, already having not lived half my day.

Parking lot dance-offs to unapproved music with the few people that had become my tribe there were the only spots of joy of my life and getting a piercing okayed by my dad was the highlight of my time there.

But the most epic moments were after a weekend visiting my friends and my boyfriend, arriving back, hungover and smelling of liquor—and then having a rude awakening as my two worlds collided. It is cold in Pennsylvania—as in, it snowed in October. So, I attempted to be slick and smoke in the shower; even a soggy cigarette would get me through until I could trudge up my freedom hill. The bathroom would be full of smoke and Febreze fumes and I would step out wondering just who would catch on, who knew and wasn't telling me.

The next morning the house mom came to my room and asked if she could talk. Uh, sure. She told me someone had found a cigarette in the toilet and brought to her attention that I was the last in the bathroom that evening. First of all, I thought, Gross—that's some serious business if someone put their hand in the toilet to tattle. Secondly, my dad was going to love that his daughter was once again the one causing havoc. I told her that the friends I'd been with for the previous few days smoked and their cigarettes were in my suitcase, so I had to dispose of them. She looked at me, nodding, and I was absolutely sure she did not believe one word I said.

I didn't have a car, so I got a ride to Kroger to get rid of my cigarettes. No way I was throwing those bad boys out anywhere around where people would dig for things anywhere.

This swift run to the grocery store to unload all things nicotine in secret epitomized my inability to even begin to belong in this bubble of toilet divers and skirt measurers. I wanted to flee, but I also felt shame again for not belonging, and I felt a further disconnect from a relationship I didn't even know if I wanted to be connected with: God. I was more with-drawn, from nicotine and from my escape-artist self. My escape, which felt like where I belonged, where I made sense, and where I felt peace, felt like it just got tossed in the Kroger trash can.

The only beauty I found was in the few friends I had... those who sat on the steps with me and shared life with me—with room for Jesus, of course—and who danced with me in parks in a way Baptists don't dance, the ones that knew of my relationships and joined the secret Skype sessions I had in my room with my people in Kentucky and other schools, despite the fact that Skype was forbidden. They were the ones who hung out virtually, the ones who had taken the trudge up the hill to sit with me as I smoked just to show that their loyalty was with who I was, not with who everyone wanted me to be.

NASCAR Jesus

So, at this point in my grind, Jesus felt like Febreze and a pack of gum and drowning in Bath and Body Works lotion in order to feel worthy enough to be seen and heard.

Me and Jesus were like NASCAR-ing it. Like those races, which are all about speed and who crosses the finish line first, me and Jesus were turbulent, fierce and loud going from one high emotion to the other. We had no middle ground. I either believed completely or wanted nothing to do with him.

Every time I felt a nudge or peace from something bigger than myself, someone dug a cigarette out of the toilet of my life. Like for real, bro. I just thought I saw a glimpse of something I could marvel at and then I was just back smoking uphill.

People were my Jesus buzz kills but they also showed me Jesus by choosing to trudge with me and be present with me. Jesus showed up every time in my trenches, in my uphill smokes and moments on my knees in surrender.

I didn't surrender in a church or our daily required services or devotionals—not even within the words of the many Bibles I had with my name carved in the binding. My Jesus only allowed himself to be seen in genuine epic and dynamite humans and in my trenches and within the faces of those who Febreze-d it up and sat and waited in the car for me after I took the puffs I needed to recollect myself and take my mask off.

The people I saw and witnessed Jesus in were those who saw me in the midst of my trenches—and brought a flashlight.

"I'll sit with you here, Jaydee," they'd say, "but I'm not letting you stay here. Let's go."

Last Call

This school was an incredibly bad idea. They thought if they prayed and chapeled me enough, I would be saved. I promised I would try it for one semester, for the free education my father's employment gave me and for the slight chance we might become family again. I wanted one last attempt to connect with this man who biologically was my father.

One night, the depression and loneliness were overwhelming. All of it was colliding at once and I could not contain it any longer. Weeping and wanting to cut myself, I called to ask my dad if I could come see him and talk. I ran down the hill to finally confide, to finally have father and daughter sacred time, to finally be seen and embraced and to hear that I was loved and it was all going to be all right.

I walked into the room where he was living on campus and it felt so weird, like he was an adult living the dorm life that somehow had hotel vibes. This was the place he stayed when he wasn't home, which was most of the time. I was seeing this life was for staying away from my mom, staying away from us, from married life and family life—a small hotel-type room with a microwave, with clothes hanging on the back of a chair and shoes and workout clothes spread out across the bed. Clearly, he was trying to act like he was 30 again and had to have a body to go with the glances he threw any woman's way.

I began to let my feelings loose and I saw coldness.

I saw a head shake of disappointment.

I saw a look of judgment.

I needed to get over it.

Then this small space made sense.

The life away from life made sense.

The life he didn't face made sense.

The way he numbed himself made sense.

And I realized I had been hustling for a man to see me who didn't even see himself.

I had been hustling for my worth with a man who held a label that tugged so deeply at me. It pulled on me in times when I needed to lean on someone who was supposed to uphold his honor by raising me. The label was "father."

When I realized I was trying to be seen by someone who didn't see himself, I realized, through tears, the reality: that I was just like the disposable little microwave.

There was no warmth in this space, no consistency, no warm arms of an embrace.

I looked at my dad's face, hoping he would understand I

was hurting and want to help me find a direction, an answer —or just tell me I would get through it.

"I'm so depressed," I told him. "So unhappy. I've been, you know, back to old habits. I'm trying so hard, but it's hard to live and breathe here."

He looked at me and I went cold. My stomach sank. I knew it was just like every other conversation.

A smirk, laughter.

"Oh please. You're fine. Get it together," he said.

I went home and wept from the deepest part of myself. I don't know if it was sadness about being stuck where I was, homesickness, the knowledge that I was unable to be someone other than I was or the deep reality that even behind my "don't mess with me face," I had still hoped that a relationship I pretended I didn't want would mend.

I climbed into bed feeling my fakeness, my willingness to hustle to be someone others wanted me to be. But all I really wanted was to just be able to be broken.

Did he break me more that night?

Or did I just finally allow myself to break open?

After the one semester I had promised, my mom kept her word and I was on my way home. With snow heavily falling on the ground, I said my goodbyes. I hugged it out with the people who had become my people during this chapter of my life, not quite realizing how deeply I had sunk into my trenches and into depression.

Fake IDs and Photos

Nothing healed. Nothing mended. I felt nothing except for the feeling that I was about to burst wide open.

I was ready to box out of all the restrictions. It was my time to do life the way I wanted to and I wasn't going to be hiking up any hills to do that.

I was going to be relentless and bold and unreserved.

Back home, back with an old boyfriend, back with the crew, I was trying to hustle and re-engage after being gone. I was back to drinking and smoking whenever I pleased, reconnecting with all my old sources and escapes.

My parents went out of town together, an almost unheard-of trip to the beach. And I finally had free reign of the home I grew up in—a space, a place, a fake ID and the perfect scenario to act out what was in me, what others deemed a rebellion.

I was on my last straw with them. One more incident and I was *out*.

Our basement had never been so packed with cards, booze and members of the opposite sex.

Early in the night, we peaced out with the knowledge that we would pick up the next day. Parents weren't coming home yet.

A digital camera was left on the wicker table in the middle of many packs of Bud Light. It was full of photos of tipsy laughter and kissy faces and chug contests and cards sprawled on the transparent table, which showed the confetti black floor my mom had picked out. She was so intentional with every color, every piece of decor and every detail of this lifeless home. The colors on the wall kept the home warm, but the hearts within it failed to match its lively vibes.

While my sister was always my foundation, handing me my running shoes when I needed to be forced out of my feels and onto the pavement, she was also my tattle tale—telling the truth of what I never wanted to face or fight.

When she found the digital camera, she scrolled until she had seen enough. Shocker—Jaydee had once again broken the rules.

She gave me the "Either I'm going to tell them or you are" talk.

Well, I sure as heck was not going to. Duh.

I was on my last leg there, already knew I was about to be on the road. Instead of calling them, I packed up.

I didn't want to be thrown out. I just wanted to party. I wasn't ready to stay for the fight, to be humbled or have the tough conversations.

I just wanted to toss a garbage bag full of crap in my friend's car and go.

I left for good.

9

Out

A friend and her family took me in.

At this point, three amazing families had taken me in at different times in my life. They had loved me and supported me.

They allowed me to be lost and pretend to be found at the same time.

They provided a haven where I could be messily seen and loved and cared for in a way that was not possible in my own home. They knew this and never hesitated to let me crash at their homes at any hour or even tell me when I'd have to leave.

I sat on my friend's mattress one day, alone in the home while she was off in cosmetology school. I considered my life, thinking "WTF am I doing" while also wrestling with whether I should fight for my boyfriend after cheating on him at a party. That's when I realized I had been doing absolutely nothing with my life.

What did I even want to do? I couldn't sit waiting for my friend to come back so we could cram hummus and play beer pong. I couldn't drink and hit the road for the rest of my life.

My friend was doing something with her life, as were other

people my age. There had to be more to life for me. I had to find a way to get out of my world and into another. I wanted so deeply to leave my own self that I thought finding a new version of myself was the answer—that it would fix this, make me feel better, free me from my mess of a life.

Between beers or sitting and chain-smoking, I had thoughts. In those moments or lying in bed at night, I dreamed. I thought of helping people. I thought of writing and investing in girls and women. I thought of younger versions of me and versions of me that were in the same spot I was. I thought of what it would be like if I could do something bigger with my life.

So one day, I quit numbingly dreaming and I decided to do something.

I got on the phone with a college adviser who helped me get everything set up to go rock out the college experience I had wanted so badly. Taking her time, she helped with housing, aid, FAFSA and funding. After countless phone calls and emails, she fired me off into a new chapter of my life.

My friend helped me load my crap back in her car. I thanked her epic family and I was on my way. We stopped for a fresh nose piercing and then she dropped me off to my new escape route.

Dorm Life

I took my stuff up to a door and opened it to find someone else all settled in. Several photos were on the shelves and I couldn't tell which ones featured her. But none of them were anything like the 11th-floor Harry Potter fan I was first assigned to. I had told the front desk I couldn't bunk with her because I was scared of heights. Yeah, I'm not scared of heights. I'm just not a fan of Harry Potter posters all over my room. I preferred someone who was cool with sneaking booze into the mini fridge and smoking out the window with Rihanna playing.

The second roommate, a Mustang-driving, dark-headed, fierce and goofy human, became my person—my lifeline through this crazy chapter.

This new school was the polar opposite of the other, where I was shunned for wearing purple pants and had a mandated distance from the opposite sex. Things were a tad different: frat parties, beer pong, makeout seshes in hallways and across campus and white trash bash parties where we made outfits solely out of a trash bag. I killed that. At this public university, they also had no intention of making sure my bed was made or that I attended class. So, in most cases, neither happened.

It wasn't all perfect. One day, I had to blame my toasted hair dryer for causing smoke to seep into the upper floor dorm rooms—once again, people tattle-telling on my perfectly normal habit of smoking indoors. What was up with those people? Jeez.

Many nights I fell asleep numb on my upper bunk. I crash-landed out of drunkenness and rattled my roomie early in the AM with tunes to pump me up on my way to class. She was my go-to soul for revving up the car engine in the snow to get cigarettes and for bundling up and heading outside to indulge a nicotine craving. She would always be down to set up beer pong in the dorm room whenever I could get her to stay the weekend instead of heading home to be with her boyfriend. She was a surprise in this new chapter and a nonjudgmental safety zone for my recklessness.

Our crew began to extend down the hallway on our floor. We all became each other's people. We began to love each other in the midst of learning to love and learn about ourselves.

I got the nickname "Little Momma" from one of my dearest friends, who took legit care of my drunkenness way too many times. Each time I busted my face, broke my nose or crashed into some other drunken mistake, I would end up cuddled in my bed because her angelic self somehow got me in my room safely and up to the top bunk once again.

People have constantly been my crash pad

My mattress in the middle of running

My blown-out hairdryer in the midst of getting kicked out for smoking

My safety in turbulent times

My confessions about my cutting

My back-road riding, Marlboro-buying, song-mixing people

My "accepted people"

My letter exchanges in treatment

My "phone a friend" in times of need

My "I'll go get your car" or "Come pick you up"

My place to vent and disclose the pain that showed up the next morning

My borrowed phones when I needed to text my boyfriend because my phone was taken away [BY WHO?]

My people who were honest with me when life was really painful

My reciprocal people, the ones who loved and leaned and allowed me to do the same

My people who saw the numb, messy and unapologetic me and helped me feel seen

My top bunk bed in the midst of face-planting

My "You can do better" in the midst of settling

My family in the midst of being disconnected from mine

My safety when life and my inner state felt like war

My get-out-of-jail-free card

My resiliency factors

My crew, my people

High Life

In the midst of finding my people and attempting to find myself, I also found a lot of parties.

Shortly after getting to school, I was on academic probation and losing my financial aid. My parents were not co-signing since they knew I wouldn't be attending classes so much as using the meal card for Subway and smoothies galore.

My studies consisted of: Which party can I crash and how much can I drink before I get there?

I never missed a day at the gym. I loved that place.

I rocked out running, attempted lifting and socialized.

I was hard on my body, but at this point, I still could love my body. I could see myself and direct my thoughts toward realism and past the shame I threw at it—the comparison, the self-doubt...maybe some carryover from a younger age when I got breasts late. I could sweat and feel good. I could work out next to a girl with rock-hard abs and a cute, perfectly styled ponytail and makeup and still feel pretty badass myself.

I would put out my cigarette right outside the gym and head on in for a few hours. I was relentless in my determination to just not give an f.

I would run around campus and feel so good walking up the freaking massively long hill to the classes I didn't pay attention to.

I began hanging with the frat boys, going to the frat parties. I was invited to their formals, though the only one I remembered was where I fell in gravel and my tooth went through my lip and my nose broke because I could never rock any type of heel, sober or not.

I had regular weekend stomping grounds and a crew—places, parties, booze and shots, themed nights and selfies. I blacked out more times than I could count and I had recklessly horrible nights and mornings I wished I could remember and yet didn't want to remember. I never wanted to think about it all on my walk of shame home or as I stumbled to the community bathrooms after staggering out of bed. I would get so hungover I didn't make it to class.

My body felt like a free-for-all and many nights some frat boy would send a sober pledge to pick me up. Where there was booze, there I went.

At this point, I justified everything with "I do what I want and I don't care what anyone thinks about it." I would get the drunkest of the drunk, make out on the dance floor, dance all up on the stage, hear about it the next day and say, "And?"

I still wasn't getting the calls back after the one-night stands or makeouts at parties and bars. I still would lie awake at night and know I wanted to find a way home but think, "I fought for this rebellion, I fought for this freedom, I fought for this life." I wasn't going to leave it and I for damn sure wasn't going to tell anyone I wanted out of it.

I just kept telling myself, "This is me."

White Trash Bash

It was a Wednesday night and I had a Thursday morning class.

Did I study? No.

Did I think about it for a minute? Yes, a minute.

Did I instead just find a shirt I could rip up in "white trash" style and get markers and paint up my arms with fake tats and tease my hair?

Uh, yes, yes, I did.

I honestly never said no to a party.

If I had an invite—it could've been just to hang out with two people—I was there.

This night, none of my friends wanted to go out, so I persisted.

I knew some of the people there so I decided I would just meet up with all of them.

Dress up and get trashed? Sign me up.

I walked into that night knowing I was going in with *zero* plans.

Zero plans of getting home, zero plans of where to even put my things, zero plans of how much I planned to drink and had zero plans of who I could crash with.

That night had rebellious vibes for me.

I drank into oblivion.

The next morning, I had a final exam.

I really needed to pass at least one class.

I had already dropped the majority of them.

Somehow, I crash-landed back in my dorm room, on my roommate's bed with no sheets on it. She had moved out already because it was the end of the semester.

I was smeared with tats I made and a few new ones with boys' names, my teased hair a fight in itself, reeking of spilled beer and shots. And I was still in my Daisy Dukes and ripped-up red T-shirt.

The next thing I knew, someone was banging on my door.

This banging was my mother who drove in the middle of the night to rattle my drunk self up to go to my final—legit got out of bed and drove an hour-and-a-half.

I think she was worried I wasn't alive.

Ya see, unknown to me, in the midst of my drunkenness, I would call her.

I would tell her I wanted to die, that I knew I was a big ol' screwup and I drink so much I put myself in God-awful situations.

Remember when I left?

Yeah, I left her and when I mean left I didn't speak to anyone in my family any longer.

They didn't know where I was, who I was with or what I did with my life.

So, the only glimpses she saw were my 4 am blackout phone calls.

That I honestly didn't know occurred.

That morning, she powered past the check-in where you have to show your ID and your guest has to come to check you in and she told them she *was* going to go up to my room to wake me up.

I had not seen my mom in a long time.

I was shocked in a "WTF must I have said to her last night" way.

She looked at me and hurried me, tats and all, to just change clothes and run to my final.

She knew with all her soul I could for real probably not recall my name at that point.

But she so badly just wanted me to show up for myself.

I didn't have my phone, my ID or my purse.

She told me where she would be waiting for me.

I sat in the class where the teacher always left the door open for me.

Nodding in and out and inhaling cigarette smoke residue from my hair and shaking my head as I re-discovered all my ridiculous new markered tattoos.

After moving my pencil back and forth and scribbling some bubbles, I left the class, feeling like I was going to puke. I slid down the icy cold cement wall to crash on the floor for a moment before getting up and walking back to look my mom in the eyes.

Everything was still very foggy.

Realizing, my mom may know the hole in my soul.

The feelings I rock of being used, being seen and not validated, being lonely and at times so drunk I feared for my own life, not knowing what happened to me or what might have transpired that I didn't know about.

How do I look at her?

I didn't even want to be seen, but yet so badly I did.

She looked at me and asked, "How did you do?" even when she knew the answer.

I told her I didn't think I got one answer right.

And I sighed a bit and told her this was the only class I liked because my professor always left the door open for me. Always.

She always nudged me to speak and ask and I was validated.

We talked about the world in there, feels and the reality of how a lot of it is unjust.

We shared ideas and opinions and we learned about each other.

She left the door open for my stumbling self just because I think she saw I loved it, too.

I somehow got a D and she was one of the first professors I told I think I want to be a social worker.

One of the only credits I took with me.

My mom nodded and said, "You showed up."

And right then, that meant so much to the both of us.

Broke

The next summer, I forced myself to surrender to landing back in the family house, though I sought a fresh vibe in my sister's room and took it over for the summer.

Psh, my father was not at all thrilled with me being back in his crib.

Nor was he a fan of me at all. Still.

That was a recurring theme.

He quietly gritted his teeth, shook his head and dismissed my presence.

He made remarks about my inability to do anything with my life, threw the phone book in front of me and told me to start calling.

I wasn't going to occupy space in his home without bringing in money.

I wasn't going to "sleep around" and "party" on his bill.

I ventured to a strip of bars in downtown Louisville.

Maybe I could get in while I was still underage and also make mad money.

I dressed in business attire and walked from pub to pub trying to figure out where I could make the most dough.

I walked into a tavern at age 19 and was hired on the spot—a hostess with a promise to be a waitress once I turned 20.

The manager asked what my availability was.

"*Wide open*. Please work me every single day and hour of my life."

She did not hesitate to fulfill this request and I began to work doubles. Every single day.

I began to find a grind, find my people of the summer and form relationships that revolved around the crap I cared about: smoking, drinking, fun and late and long hours.

We all had our demons and our struggles and we all meshed so messily.

After I turned 20, the restaurant's general manager, who wanted to help me make more money, walked me to the bar down the strip. Introduced to the staff, I was made a "howler," a cocktail waitress.

I worked doubles as often as I could. I began on that street in the morning with people who lived downtown strolling by and lawyers and workers in suits grabbing their coffees. I waitressed the lunch shift, cranked out half of the dinner shift and then changed in the bathroom and headed to serve cocktails until two or three in the morning. Then I swiped a row of shots and finished off my night, driving home intoxicated as the strobe lights were rocking, the streets were lively and loud and the drunkenness was at closing time levels—friends leaning on one another, security escorting some and others laughing and dancing and drinking until they couldn't anymore.

It became a lifestyle: work all night, party all night, sleep all day and grind on.

All of my people were on the same schedule and we all grinded the same way.

I was making good money, had a whole new crew of friends and was set to fund my own car by summer's end so I could go back to school.

Once again, these people had mad love for me, wanted me to shoot for the stars, saw my struggle, saw my partying as just part of me and they just loved me all the way up in it—as they were all up in it as well.

These people begged me not to drive home, made me text them when I got there, had countless shots and cigarette breaks with me. They walked with me in the parking garage and goofed off with me on long shifts. They got up in random homes with me in the wee hours of the morning after we legit partied until the sun came up, making memories I will prob never be able to fully recall. I would get up and try to find my phone and call whoever would pick my wandering around and hungover self up and drop me off somewhere to sleep and shower off the booze and smoke and hungoverness.

I was never home, always working or sleeping, and when my dad would accuse me of doing a dirty, slutty, no-good job, I would whip out the wads of dollar bills from my pockets and he would grow silent.

I would slip out of my parents' house for my shifts in tight clothes, booty shorts, my boosted and padded bra and loads of makeup, ready to crank out some money from drunken men who called me Jade and tried to sloppily make their moves on me after I dropped off their buckets of beer or lemonade Hurricanes. I laughed and flipped my hair and entertained them, giving them the best nights out they ever had.

I was a damn good waitress.

But I knew I would have to get out. I knew the summer would end. I was on academic probation at school from not attending or doing any work. My housing wasn't covered, so I called and called and called to snag an interview with an apartment complex. My parents sure wouldn't sign anything for my wild self. My only in? To work there.

I was the proud owner of a small green Ford Focus and had an interview. I headed to Bowling Green to find a place to work and live so I could go back to the university part time the following semester.

I drove up and stepped onto the property that would forever change my life.

I interviewed and got the job on the spot.

This secured my employment and my apartment, and all my girls were going to live with me there.

I headed home for a few more weeks to party, grind and save some more money to make it through life back at the university.

My employment at the apartment complex would pay for my rent but not give me anything extra, so I needed to shore up my cash supply.

The bar agreed to let me come back to work one weekend a month so I would have enough to stay afloat.

I said bye to my summer homies and moved into a four-bedroom apartment to wait for my girls.

I had also found my soul sister and beyond, my ride-or-die girl who would be with me through this next messy chapter of my life. She was also there to get her apartment paid for. I trained her to show apartments and after one day, we were smoking cigarettes on our breaks together and realizing we would love this job simply because we'd get to chill together. We looked forward to working together and giving ridiculous tours of model units and using the tanning beds as much as we pleased. And we realized we needed one another outside of work, too. We always collided, always connected and were always there for one another. She was the one that always had my back.

She and I and the other staff worked during move-in week. Not only was I able to welcome every new tenant, but I also welcomed all my humans into our apartment. My previous roommate and another friend lived in one unit and my three other roomies and I were just on the other end of the complex. We were so incredibly hyped to have our freedom, our own space and our own place to party. Together again.

Fake IDs, wine and Keystone beer 30-packs were forever in our apartment. We never really turned it off or chose to stop, partying day, night, morning, sunrise, sunshine.

I worked, partied, tried to school and repeated.

10

Jade

Life was a non-stop party with smoke breaks in between.

One weekday evening, soon after getting all moved in, one of my roommates and I headed across the complex. We were moving our weekday party to our friends' apartment. We decided to turn the beginning of the week into a wild night of drinking, laughing and an epic beer pong battle.

Someone came into my friends' apartment and asked, "You're Jade, right?"

I looked over and saw a man without a shirt and he was double-fisting some beers.

I said yes warily as I stepped back to pick up the ping pong ball and toss it into a red solo cup. I looked at my friends and said it was weird that he knew my name and I didn't even know of his existence, but maybe I had seen him at the gym.

He went back upstairs and one of my guy friends followed him and hollered down the steps, "He thinks you're hot." My mind shifted from "Creepy, this dude knows me" to "Hmmm, what's he all about?"

My thoughts began to play a game within themselves. "Maybe it's not that creepy. Maybe he just noticed me. It's good to be noticed, right?"

Someone told me that this dude grinded like I did in the gym and I soon found out he had asked people there who I was. He was obviously used to asking around when he saw something that interested him.

Eventually, I remembered seeing him there. Something was cooking before I could have fathomed he had a plan for me—a young, reckless soul lost in her own mess of a life.

He saw a body, a blonde, blue eyes, fit and unapologetic, a partying being he could choose to make his.

I had no idea how deeply I was about to lose myself. I would enter a game I should have never begun.

The night of the weekday party, I was wearing jeans and a black V-neck. My hair was curled and I looked like a tipsy-good Monday night drunk.

I didn't know this night would change my life, rock my world and cause everything I knew to shift. The woman who was there that night would never be present again.

It was the beginning of one of my muckiest trench dives, a dive I sometimes allowed myself to wallow in, a space where sometimes I had no idea how deeply I was in. At times, I believed it was the only place on Earth I was worthy of being in.

I had been wandering for quite some time, experimenting, allowing men to take me home and not care what happened to me or where I went the next morning.

I was used to walking past people on campus who I knew, knew me and my body, who tried to take advantage of me or did and who mocked me and who enjoyed me in my drunken stupors, because they benefited from my numb slumber.

This dude and I met in this numbness.

He found me in a state of my life that, at times, I walked out of and then felt helpless, lost and so broken and small that I would turn back around and wade right back in.

A place that made me homesick when I left it, but I felt as though it was caked on me like dried mud.

And I couldn't shake it, nor could I show anyone I was "free or clean or new."

It became a constant stain, a constant pain and a constant state of feeling.

I was sinking deeper and deeper in muck.

I just ended up surrendering all the way in, completely losing all of me and silencing myself and not asking for help.

No fight left, allowing it to just surround me and cling to me. Maybe if I didn't budge it wouldn't be so hard to breathe.

Dating

I stumbled away from the party that night and went home with my friends. This dude and I kissed before we went our separate ways and I had the lingering thought that this could be a fling or we could be more than friends, even though we had only shared space for a few hours.

I had told him that I had to wake up early to go to work and asked him to check in to ensure I got up. I thought this would be a smooth way to exchange numbers.

The next morning, hungover, I woke up to more than 30 calls and texts reminding me I had to get up to work, to text him and call him back.

His name repeated all over my call log and text after text all over the screen of my phone. I was surprised he had remembered. I mean, that was progress from my long list of "no calls after walk of shame back home."

Sweet, right? Oh, he "checked in."

After my shift at work, he landed right on my couch, with me cuddled right up next to him.

And after that day, he never left.

Very quickly, my body was his, my mind was his and my every move needed to be accounted for. From there, he was the only one coming through on my cell phone.

One night not long after we had met, I was leaving my

girlfriend's apartment and walked down the hallway to the metal stairs that led to both the upper and lower floors.

My friend and I had just been rocking to Lil Wayne and making our way through our playlist to the sounds of Owl City. The Percocets had just begun hitting us when I saw the dude walking up the stairs, gym bag on his shoulder and a red bandana on his head, straight from his workout, to sit with me on the steps outside my girlfriend's unit. He lived just one floor up.

He looked at me and told me our relationship was Facebook official or it was nothing. I needed to commit publicly or he had other options. I wasn't ready to commit. We had only known each other for a few days.

I liked him, it was fun, but Facebook official? Nope. I didn't roll like that.

I laughed. Psh. But as he rose up and headed upstairs, I began to feel the rise of what I soon felt every day: shame, worry and the hustle to not be replaced.

"Well, should I just do that?" I wondered.

"Well, am I lucky to have him?"

"Well, should I just date him because he could just as easily go get someone else?"

"Well, I wanted to be single, but maybe I don't. Maybe he's it and I can't let it go."

"Was that controlling? Did he just give me an ultimatum or does he just really like me?"

"Are these other girls just his friends? If I come in, do they go away or stay?"

"Do I need to just go up there and make this all better?"

"Do I need to post about him more on Facebook?"

"Am I just being too slow and just not showing him I want him enough?"

The rattling of those feels grew as time went on. My thought processes became so different. I sat with these thoughts and feelings. I shuffled them into different compartments and justified some and thought some were stupid.

I was still able to separate what was mine and what was his, with my desire for independence and a voice still intact. I made decisions, even the worst of them, with my head held high and not caring what anyone thought of them.

These shifts, these rattles were new to me and had me questioning myself.

At that point, I didn't know what a true committed relationship looked like.

So maybe this was a thing? Maybe I was just being stubborn?

Maybe I should've asked some questions on those lame notecards back in high school sex ed, since I was sitting at the age of 19 with still no clue what all this relationship stuff was supposed to look like.

There I went. Facebook official it was.

After only knowing him a week.

Things were going at a rapid speed. I couldn't keep up, though something in me was determined to be enough to not be replaced, to impress him, to be without fault and above criticism.

Soon, every time he yelled, punched a hole in the door, abandoned me or was abusive to me, apologies started coming in the form of lingerie—a gift more to himself. Sex turned into public knowledge. My body was everyone's business and so was my performance in bed.

The gym was no longer my sanctuary but a demand, as my body was critiqued to the last inch and I felt I needed to compete with the bodies of all the women around me, around him.

The males in my life, gone. Other humans' texts coming into my phone, gone.

Then the photos of me began.

I remember the first few times feeling sexy and glamorous.

I wanted to send them. I waited anxiously for the response.

Then I remember the next 5,000 after that.

And each time a pit grew in my stomach as I read "a little lower" when I sent photos of my face, realizing he didn't care about that.

That rattled inside me to my core.

It wasn't glamorous or sexy anymore. It was a chore.

One day, I was hunched over his computer, alone where I normally sat the opposite way of him, straddling and hugging him as he typed, and I saw a folder on his computer with tiled photos.

I double-clicked the folder and found women, their body parts staring back at me. An instant gut-wrenching pit opened in my stomach. It wasn't porn. Well, it was, but these women weren't actors. They were women just like me.

Why does he even need me? I wondered. So many shapes and sizes. Comparisons and pain rushed through me like a shot of adrenaline. I was sick. I was torn and self-conscious. Why are you having me send pictures if you have an album of these women? Did I get added to the tab?

I was yelling, full of disbelief and shame that I would never be enough as I scanned these bodies and then thought of myself.

I couldn't marvel at a woman's beauty anymore. I only saw her and thought of him secretly with his eyes undressing her. I saw her beauty and discounted mine. I saw her features and began to degrade mine and I saw her and thought of that folder.

"You're crazy, stop being crazy and overexaggerating," he said. "All guys do this. Get over it."

Nothing was deleted. And I stayed there to resume my duties as the woman outside of this folder.

But I felt that these women were more seen and more important than me.

I heard his voice in my head when I looked at my body and though I wanted to dismiss it, his voice lingered and shouted when I undressed and when I looked at myself. I hated it, but the most painful part was I believed it. It became my voice. It was me.

I had become conditioned to perform, to play a part and I was more concerned about what I looked like without clothes on than with them.

I was conditioned to always know it was coming, always know I wasn't going to be cuddled or hugged without giving something in return.

I did what I had to. I flipped a switch to function and get through. I was not involved in anything intimate. I was performing. I sent the photos. I surprised him with lingerie. I did what I felt he wanted me to do and I tiptoed around anything other than that.

I didn't want him to leave and I also knew he didn't see me as enough to stay for because he often did leave. My body was my only bargaining chip. If I didn't do it, then I would lose, I would be unwanted, I would be left and replaced.

He wrecked my soul in what seemed the hardest and most intimate ways to untangle and rewire. Psychologically, mentally, emotionally and physically.

My worthiness was intertwined with my ability to "get the job done" and not who I *was*.

I began to drink into oblivion again, giving him plenty of reasons to break up with me over and over. When I drank, I blacked out. I would act a mess and give him all the opportunity to "be mad at me" and "want nothing to do with me," which meant him also doing whatever he wanted for the next few days.

Then, when he would decide to talk to me again, I would get a text from my roommates that said he was walking over.

And the next thing I knew, my depressed self in bed heard the door slam, the door with the holes from all his kicking when he was angry, the door I got maintenance to replace over and over after I said it was damaged at a party.

That door would open and he would crawl into bed and say "I'm sorry" once again.

Domestic violence literature refers to the honeymoon phase, which is a part of the grooming process to entice, lure and manipulate a partner and to cause them to commit and fall for the individual.

This was no honeymoon phase.

No, this was real-deal dangerous from Day One.

I just had no idea it could be so incredibly mind-warping, confusing and addicting.

Weekends at His Family's Home

I had completely disconnected from my family. I was a loner intentionally.

They would try to check in and I would ignore them again and again. For months. I was deeply ashamed, thinking, "What do I even say?"

They knew I was dating someone from what they saw on social media, but I had no words to describe it. It was hard to talk about someone who walked out one day and loved me the next.

What was the point of trying to describe it or defend it or acknowledge it when half the time I didn't know what it was or wasn't or if it would be on or off?

I knew it wasn't something I could glorify. I didn't even still know why I was doing it. My family already knew I was a screwup. So, I refrained from telling them anything, from talking to them at all.

Even in my loneliest of moments, I just couldn't muster up the energy to call. I didn't know what I was all the way lost and engulfed in. And I didn't have the energy to defend it.

My friends and this life were everything for me.

I was packing up for my weekend back at bar life to make ends meet and now this dude and I went everywhere together.

And because I had no connection to my family at this point, I needed a place to crash-land after my shifts, so I stayed at his family's house.

I remember the time we had driven my car, pulled up to the house and a bing went off on my phone.

"What the f?" he yelled, getting out of the car. "Forget it. Just find somewhere else to go. You're not staying with me."

He went inside.

And I had nowhere to go.

I called up my person, the person whose mattress I had crash-landed on before I had left for Western Kentucky University and asked for the favor again.

.

"We had a little, you know, thing," I said. "He just needs to cool off. Can I just chill at your place, have a beer, smoke a few and get ready to go in?"

"You bet. Come on over," she said.

When I got there, I sank into her bed and puffed through a bunch of cigarettes before getting dressed for a long night at work.

Around 1 am while I was still at work, he texted me to just come in the back door.

"I can stay with him," I texted my friend. "I don't need to crash."

I closed the bar and headed that way, even though this dude had disappeared and left me feeling small and shameful once again. For nothing.

If I had stayed with my person, he wouldn't know where I was. He didn't tolerate not knowing where I stayed or who I was with. It was easier to avoid the rage, avoid the violent name-calling, all of which just ensured I would be where he wanted me when he wanted me there.

The Morning After

The next day before my evening shift, we went to a flea market, holding hands. He acted like he had done nothing bad to me the day before.

We stopped in front of a woman with several tiny, malnourished kittens. So many and so cute yet so sad. There was a story behind these furballs. The woman told us they had been buried alive and left for dead.

"We need this," he said to me, even though he didn't have any money of his own to take care of a cat. But we handed over 10 bucks and next thing you know, we HAD this constantly meowing and helpless black and white kitten in our arms.

Maxy was an attempt to try to make things "right," make a good memory out of all this bullshit and toxicity.

Maxy slept in my hair and cried all night. Her litter box was in the folding closet door of my apartment and her presence was like glue, something that bound this dude and I more tightly, made us feel like we were okay.

I kept these short moments close to me. I held on to them when I needed to battle with myself about why I shouldn't leave him.

I could say "We were happy," " He makes me laugh" and "It's great."

Every single time someone would ask how things were with us, I tried to cling to these memories because I knew that they were so few. And I was hustling to make people like us, make them think we were a good pair, make them think it was worth it for me to go back time and time again.

But people saw. Everyone saw. They saw him yelling at me and demeaning me. They knew he left, came back over and over and I let him.

I was seen, even though it mostly happened behind my back. People saw my pain and they knew that when I was curled up behind blacked-out curtains with booze galore things were not "fine," but, man, did I hustle to win them over.

Our relationship was a constant coverup and a constant stream of manipulative gifts after a huge fallout. Maxy was just the most recent attempt to make things right.

Silent Antidote

This relationship unwound toxically. I slowly became someone I hated and did not know.

I was small in all ways in my life—physically, mentally, spiritually, emotionally. I didn't know what was right or wrong anymore. I didn't know what I felt or didn't feel anymore, and I didn't know who I was or even if I wanted to find her.

I was still drinking into oblivion and my ride-or-die girl and I crushed up pills and snorted them down. Pills were back in my life in a powerful way. I began to seek them, find them and bargain for them. At times, I worried my concoctions would kill me.

I sought the freedom within them, the numbness from them, the safety of avoidance and the serenity within them. When I took them, the thoughts, the pain, the confusion and the depression felt layered and covered by film—a film that allowed me to function without breakage or the sharp reminders of what I was enmeshed in.

My people knew about the pills but this dude did not. Not yet. There were people I met up with only to get pills. He would accuse me of just about everything else and try to make sense of my calm and remote composure.

My silent escape. One that did not reek of intoxication, one that didn't seem as though I was "insane or crazy" or lost in this mess of a life. I would whip out the pill on the living room table, in my bedroom or behind a closed door at my friend's unit. I would pay my roommates or anyone for that matter to find what I was looking for.

At this point, my friends were all aware, but they didn't judge or criticize. They would be chilling on the couches around me or wandering in and out of their rooms and talking to me and checking in with me, asking me how I felt.

Thus began my season of escaping my own relationship with this dude and reality. A habit that became the only way I could sustain it. The only high or fuel I got in my relationship and also the only way I could stay in it without dying inside, though I felt empty.

I could not tolerate being touched, being talked to or being in the presence of this human who did the farthest thing from loving me, but I also wasn't sure I could make it out.

Eventually, he realized it and realized that if he brought me pills, booze, cigarettes, everything was easier. He could get what he wanted from me without a fight, without me telling him over and over I didn't want it.

I was able to do it faster and more when I had numbness raging in my blood. When it worked for him, he used it and when it didn't—he used it against me. He would shame me for using and then when he wanted me, would buy them for me and "gift" them to me.

Bring me a six-pack, find me a pill, buy me a pack of cigarettes.

He would bring those and I could make it through what he wanted and what he had me for.

The Second Ring

My ride-or-die from high school and I had a rule. We had been friends through hell and back: her family, my family, her mother, my second mom, her home, my home away from home and her voice and her words as my truth and redemptive wisdom to find solace in.

We had both moved away from our hometown and lived in different places. We always had a rule that if crap hit the fan, if things got real very fast, if there was trouble or something serious, you always called twice. Regardless of what was going on or where you were, if you got a second call you answered because that meant you were needed and it was a big need.

One night, I took a Percocet and then snorted a second. It hit me like it had never hit me before. The apartment where I got high was just across the street from mine. I made it into my car and pulled my car directly in front of my unit.

I put the car in park and repeatedly told my legs to move. Over and over again. *Move. Get out of the car.* The message was not relaying to my body. I got out my phone and did the two-ring signal and she called.

"I can't move," I said. "I went too far. I can't move my legs."

She said, "You're doing too much. You're going too far, Jaydee. You need to stop. You said you would stop. This is too far."

My legs started working and I got to my room and went into shock. My roommate came in and asked what was going on and I told her I had done it this time. I had done too much. I scared the shit out of myself and I realized I was too high.

You know when you drink too much and you land on the top of the toilet puking all night and you tell yourself you're never drinking again?

So, what do you do then?

Uh, you go out the next weekend.

After a bit, the feelings fade, we forget or choose to, until we are smack dab back in the midst of it again, and it's real all over again.

That high terrified me, but it didn't raise me up and rattle me up enough to keep me from snorting again.

I don't know if it's because I have an addictive personality or if it's because I was in a situation where the fear of going too far was better than the pain of my reality.

I still wasn't ready, didn't feel worthy of the change or worthy of the sobriety or worthy of the shift, didn't feel capable of making it nor did I even know what it looked like.

Well, this wasn't the only two-ring emergency, not the only time she picked up to hear me in a full-out panic. The next time her phone rang twice, my life was not my own.

The Rattling

I began to slide into a deep depression, cutting myself and drinking beyond oblivion. Every move made me afraid of his reaction—who spoke to me, who was on my phone, who looked at me. The constant breaking up, getting back together, breaking up, getting back together.

I began to question what was healthy and what was not, but I still leaned into the relationship, not fully knowing and not able to walk away or determine if what I felt was even real or somehow off, since I had nothing but my own history and my parents' marriage to compare it to.

My body was tired, sex was relentless.

It was loud, it was open, it was for everyone to know.

My door was shut, but he made sure we were heard.

One time his roommate walked in and apologized, but the dude just said, "No, don't stop. Keep going."

We were wrapped in a blanket, but you could tell what was happening and that I was nude.

Or when he walked out of his room every time afterwards and laughed and wanted applause from his roommates for "fucking" me.

I became a performance in a movie I wasn't even in tune with.

I was lost, numb, checking out willingly within my own life.

I loved him and it was confusing.

I didn't know what relationships or love should look like.

I felt I owed him everything.

I felt obligated to give everything—all details, all plans, all numbers, all of my body and thoughts and texts and calls and *everything*.

I felt I had no choice but to give it all up, all of me.

And I walked around wondering what else I needed to say or give.

We had now been dating a little more than two months.

It felt like a lifetime.

Pregnancy

Fall was my absolute favorite season—the chilly wind, the leaves on the ground, the need to wear a jacket and boots and the rush to the car to avoid the goosebumps on your arms, the need to cuddle up under the covers and prepare for festivities with loved ones and friends, the need for booty warmers for long rides and movies in bed when it's too chilly to venture outdoors.

But it also carried such pain and knots in the deepest parts of my memory and my soul. In fall, I often got these feelings of heaviness, this ache and these waves of homesickness and nostalgia.

It was Thanksgiving break and I was so disconnected. The holiday breaks were not a chance to go to my home and to my family, but to go to places of toxicity, a place of pain where I ached to be surrounded by people in a place with food, laughter, love and booze.

That weekend was full of sex, pills, staying up late in a stupor and the deepest feeling of homesickness.

I tried new things, things I didn't want in my life.

I watched others doing it because he wanted to watch to "amp things up."

I gave myself away when I was worth more.

I tried to analyze myself because I didn't know what this knot was for.

I took pills because the booze wasn't numbing enough.

I was silent because I didn't think I had a voice anymore.

I laughed because I honestly didn't think there was much to live for.

I cried myself to sleep because I wanted so so so much more.

I stayed because I didn't think anyone else was there anymore.

I lay there because I knew if it wasn't me, it was her and her and her.

I watched porn with him because I couldn't catch up, keep up or want to perform anymore.

I was fading away because my soul had been dormant for far too long.

Why am I stuck in this darkened slumber?

Why can't I get out?

Why is numbness so temporary?

Where is my fire, my light, my joy, my soul?

Why can I not feel at home anywhere I go?

Why am I not enough?

Why doesn't this ease this pain in my chest, my soul and my heart?

Where is the freedom, the peace and the love for life?

God, do you even hear my flipping cry?

Don't you see I'm dying inside?

We spent Thanksgiving weekend in his parents' basement.

On the way home, I grabbed the "I swear I'm done after this" Marlboro Light pack for the ride, aching from within and from smiling from my "fun weekend" out.

My body ached from Plan B once again and my pockets had no money left to spare because, he said, "condoms just don't feel good." My heart was aching that I had lost connection with my own blood and couldn't embrace those I needed love from so desperately, every piece of me just wanting to hear my mother's voice but feeling far too ashamed and gone to simply just be humbled and press call, homesickness raging within my soul.

God, I've messed up. Is this what I get?!

How do I break free from all of this?

Bundling up, running to the car with my best friend to escape the cold, wanting out of my apartment to escape my truth and my reality, in the car, putting on a perfectly mixed CD. We went to Walgreens and scanned the aisles for the two-pack of pregnancy tests, one for her and one for me, grabbed a pack of peppermints to ease the pit in my stomach and the desire to feel a little bit in the festive mood.

We arrived home and went our separate ways to resume what we trekked out in the cold for.

Take a breath. Raise it to eye view.

+ Positive

Stare.

Scream.

Stare.

Scream.

Scream.

I am a mom.

The most real and terrifying inward sigh of peace and love overwhelmed me.

I'm a mom.

All I could mutter at this point was "*No no no no no no!!*"

And these words were not about this child.

It was because this child was *inside of me.*

What have I done?

I am a mess, I thought. I can barely take care of myself.

I am lifeless within my soul. I'm broken and so not even close to happy or healthy.

How could I dare bring a child into this?

My best friend came into the room, as did my other roommates, and they sat with me and also went to get several more pregnancy tests.

I gave the two-ring call to my best friend and she said, "Jaydee, this has saved your life."

I called this dude and texted him that we needed to talk.

He was at the gym and wouldn't leave even after I told him I was pregnant.

So, I put on my tennis shoes, grabbed my roommate and went to the gym.

Everything felt differently. Do I run or do I walk—what can I do?

He came and tapped on the side of my treadmill and just looked at me.

He left the gym and I was sweating and, for the first time in a long time, feeling so deeply.

I was very fearful and worried, but I was feeling these feelings and because of that I knew this was my greatest awakening.

Will It Bother You if It Is Yes?

I still was in shock, disbelief and doubt.

I booked an appointment at the university clinic. Maybe the five other tests were wrong.

After I checked in, the first thing they did was give me another dang test. The woman handing it to me said, "Will it bother you if it is yes, like the others?"

I looked at her with tears in my eyes with the bathroom door halfway open and said, "No, I'll keep it."

I sat on a table and a woman came in with pamphlets— abortion, adoption and labor and delivery.

She then ushered me to go. I walked down that hallway and I felt everyone knew I was pregnant.

I hurried to my car and rain began to pour.

It was as if the sky felt my grief and my broken openness.

I lit my last cigarette and could only take a puff before I allowed the rain to drench it.

I couldn't avoid it anymore. It felt wrong, when normally I felt nothing at all. I felt this abrupt wave of what I was doing no longer serving me. It wasn't fixing anything. If anything, it felt even heavier and weighed on me.

If I was going to do this, no pills, no alcohol, no cigarettes.

I wept as the windshield wipers began to click and I sat and sat and sat and thought about this shift, this huge awakening and life-altering shift.

I felt shame and guilt. This child had been in my belly for two months as I was pouring into my body things that this child never deserved. My running, my numbing, my sadness coated his lungs and heart and body and I had no idea of his existence.

Would this child be okay?

Would this affect him forever?

Will this be my fault?

I was also alone. In the doctor's office, in this pregnancy, in my life. I needed people. Badly.

My life had become focused only on escape.

I lifted the phone and called my friend's mom, my second mom.

I knew my parents would hate me, but did I have a chance?

After all this time, could I call my mom?

How do I even tell her?

Second Mom was honest with me. She was a young momma herself.

"Your dad will be really mad. He won't handle it well," she said. "But your mom, she loves you and she is full of love. Call her."

I had not talked to my mom in months. I called her and heard her voice, and I knew regardless of what the outcome was, I needed to tell her and I needed her to know I needed her.

"Mom, I have something to tell you...I'm pregnant."

She asked, "Are you okay...how did you know?"

"I went to the doctor alone."

We both wept.

Without hesitation, she said, "Honey, I'm so glad you kept this baby."

A moment of silence.

I heard her slide down a wall. She later told me she was at a conference.

She got quiet. Then she began to tell me how important it was to be healthy.

"I'm quitting it all," I responded.

It was a conversation of processing and opening up the ability for us to be honest with each other, where love began again.

I cannot tell you what else I felt in that moment, but I did feel love and no longer alone.

I then walked to this dude's unit, where he was asleep.

"I'm two months pregnant."

"Well, you're not keeping it. You're getting an abortion."

I now loved my tiny human fiercely.

I'm a mess, I thought. How in the world am I going to get myself together, get my life together, sober up, live right, separate myself?

I am a broken, depressed woman. I need to love this tiny human more than I love myself, so how do I even start?

I knew that it may take a ton of healing, a ton of hard times, a ton of growing up and wising up and opening up and being healthy, but I was going to be it.

This baby gave me this opportunity.

The opportunity to be who I was intended to be.

I might not have been worthy of this in my own eyes, for myself.

But this baby was worth it and therefore I could and would do and be that.

I slammed the door and roared, "*Well I'm keeping it.*"

I had decided and I didn't need anyone to tell me different.

I knew walking out of that unit that things were about to be really hard and very lonely.

I knew my body was going to change, as would everything about me.

I knew sober hurt, hurt my heart, hurt my realizations of my reality and that it would be full of emotions and feelings I couldn't fathom after avoiding them all this time.

I knew I would lose friends and I would feel left out and not the same anymore.

I knew I had to get my life together and that might mean I needed it to break even harder and fuller.

Then I could pick up the pieces and rid my life of those who no longer could be a part of my life.

But I had hope. And I had this baby.

Even in the darkest moments, I knew I would remind myself of that.

In It

One day, a roommate of mine had heard the dude yelling at me, as he often did. She had had enough.

Liquor bottle in hand, she came in swinging, yelling for him to stop and get out. I was watching but had no fight left in me as I walked past the holes in my door, which he had made, to silently slide onto a side of the couch. I pulled my sweater over my knuckles and laid my tired head on my hand as it rested on the arm of the chair and as my other hand cradled on my baby bump.

In that profound moment, I realized I had become my mom.

I resonated with her profoundly, I felt for her and I realized for the first time where her silence had come from.

I swore I would never be submissive, silent, allow someone to discount me and speak to me in a way I couldn't fathom anyone speaking to another human. As the door slammed, I wept, knowing I was her, wept accepting I was her.

But where was my Jaydee?

Where was my roar outside of my body?

Who was going to fight for me?

I had to.

And so, the rise began.

Epilogue

Dear Dad,

What's hard at times is not my upbringing. It's the effects of your addiction on my life. And that, not until many, many years had passed, did the world begin to see our lives and our truth, that our home and our family were your numbed-out battleground.

I wonder what it would've been like to look into clear eyes, have a gentle conversation with you, have you ask me what my feelings were instead of screaming at you as I was heading to slam my door yet again. But I also know how you raised me, built me into the woman I am today and how that allows me to be the social worker and momma I am.

Your addiction allows me to resonate with so many on levels some can't fathom.

My upbringing was not what was so saddening to me. It was seeing a family being torn and conflicted and hurt continually by someone who chose his addiction instead of his family.

I could say I get it now, being in the field and all, and I do but that doesn't change the sadness I feel for you, for all you have missed out on.

Phew, your children are beautiful and turned out so incredibly amazing and resilient, gifted and intelligent.

They give, they love and they offer light that you tried to dim.

They do what they love. They pursued their goals and dreams with integrity and that has nothing to do with you.

They prioritize family and they see their time together as sacred. They know the importance of their tone, their ability to apologize, to learn, to listen and to love so compassionately, which they missed from you.

They jerk at times when a glass spills at a table, feeling shame that they knocked it over. When someone asks them to find something, they feel fear creep in that they won't find it fast enough or get it right. They have worked on conflict and on their tone of voice in disagreements because all they heard was yelling and gritted teeth. They are so grateful for the men in their lives because they see how a partner can love truly and selflessly. They are very hard on themselves because they were raised in a home where they were never good enough.

But they—we—refused to believe that.

You see, a lot was mirrored for us, but we didn't need to bring any of that into our families. Nor did we have to believe we can't give to our kiddos what we yearned for and were worthy of in our own lives.

Our childhood was messy, like the days leading up to sitting in a circle with a bunch of "It makes me sad when you…" , "It makes me mad when you…" as our dad walked out the door with no intention of seeking treatment.

But you know what? We were some brave girls.

And we chose to continue to find out who we were in a messy and really hard intimate world.

So, I guess you could say we may have been raised up in chaos, but we were also raised up in resiliency and chose to lean into who we knew we were intended to be.

Jaydee

HERE I AM, 30, a social worker and a sober momma.

It hasn't been easy at all. I have fallen and gotten back up again. I fell into domestic violence and got back up again, lived in programs and utilized resources so we could thrive and be financially okay. I struggled through academics and feeling unworthy at times in the classroom and fought every day to be who I knew I was intended to be—a social worker. The "in-between-ness" is still a part of my grind that follows this book and into another (yes, there will be another).

This is nowhere near the end of us and our journey. We are still messy, still healing, still unapologetic, authentic and truthful. We are still trudging through our soul grind. I cannot wait to take you on the ride.

Uh, and yes, I keep in touch with all the amazing women I met in my trenches. These badass rebellious, creative and magical souls from my residential program are the dopest women, mommas, skaters and entrepreneurs.

They always had that in them. It was just coated under a hella lot of pain.

The dopest thing, though, is I got to witness it, their trenches.

When you're in the trenches with people, you get the honor of seeing what created the pain and the beauty of someone explaining their truth around it.

These girls, now women, will always have a sacred spot in my soul.

They helped me smile and love again.

Welcome to healing, friends. It takes ya back and forth and back again, so that your life and who you are deeply and intimately make sense.

Healing also requires, if you choose—which I did— humbling and reaching out to those you feel you need to make amends to.

I had to walk into this process knowing I may not have it reciprocated, I might receive truth and pain and I also might get responses I hadn't planned for, dreamed up or had, anxiety-ridden, prepped for. I had to go into each and every email, text, Facebook message or coffee date knowing this was for my personal healing, regardless of the response. I have been sitting in this long enough to know this is the work I need to do.

There were people and families I fled from, was not able to face, look dead in the face and speak my own humbling truth. I had abandoned and left some very important and pivotal people in my life, some of whom trudged legit with me during the toughest times of my adolescence. They all deserve some mighty awards for loving me on some of my most unlovable days.

As I'm writing this today, I'm at a coffee shop after two weeks of being off work because of an appendectomy. I've been burnt out and in need of a re-charge and came in to lean deep into surrender, into putting life on a standstill to rest and be still and heal.

I love coffee shops, something so fierce.

Ever been to a place where you don't know any of the faces, but these are "your people"?

Yup, coffee shop people are my people.

I feel so much in my energy, in my vibes, in my element within them.

I have had so many epic encounters in coffee shops, so many meetings and meetups with strangers and with people I love dearly—some amazing and soulful and impactful and humbling conversations.

And I love that you leave with the reminder of its space coated on your clothing and in your hair…if you have dyed your hair as much as I have so that it legit soaks right in, just like the after smell of a good bonfire.

We all have these spaces where our souls come alive,

whether it's church or nature or coffee shops, where we feel we can be exactly who we should be or dream to be or are striving to be.

Because in these spaces you come alive, refuel as much as you can so that outside of them you can also be just as you are and feel just as welcome and free to be.

I began writing this book to heal and within these pages I have cried, wanted to puke, felt peace and honor for who I am. I have wanted to shrink and then rise up even mightier. Our stories are us. It doesn't mean they are all glorious or pretty or easy to talk about. But they create the epicness of you.

They create spaces where you can lean into all of you, not just the shiny, sparkly feeling finished pieces, nah—I'm talking about the pieces that created you, modeled you, shaped you and had you pick up this book.

They create space to breathe, to relearn and relove the pieces you set to the side, numbed out and shamed or that others have shamed. Welcome her/him out, say "Hey, tell me your story" and get to know yourself again.

Those pieces have epic awakenings written all over them. The days you wept, cried, groveled and almost ended life are pieces that are trying to be heard, understood and seen so they can begin healing, so all your other pieces can begin healing, too.

Pull up a chair, fill up that coffee mug and whip out your computer or your journal and say to yourself, "Fierce one, talk trenches to me. Let's soul grind."

Acknowledgments

To Mom: You are the most selfless and loving person I know. I have seen you both in your depths and in your silence and I've been now able to witness your joy and your rise. I am here, without a doubt, because you loved me relentlessly. I cannot thank you enough for loving me in places where I felt deemed "unloveable" and a "lost cause." You are the first to cheer for me, love on me and to sit in the audience before me as I speak my truth even when each word is so close to home for you. I love you so much and you truly are my person. Thank you for not only living through this life with me but also empowering me to share it. Those days were not in vain. Momma, I love you.

To Jewel: I want to thank you for being there for me when I was a growing little girl, for allowing me to feel security and safety in your bed or arms.

To Jo: You are my inspiration and my dearest friend. You give me fierce love and accountability. You've loved me enough to rattle me when necessary and to hold me when you knew I was too broken inside to fight. You are intentional and each word, gift, note and moment spent with you is sacred and has helped me believe I'm worthy of being who I desired to be, even when I wasn't ready and didn't feel strong enough to be there. I know my journey, my decisions and my pain also affected your life. Thank you for never giving up on me and for inspiring me to be a woman who loves, gives, builds, creates and listens long enough to learn. I love you.

To My Bear: You ask, "I'm more in the next book, right?" Yes, but I need you to know there wouldn't be a story to tell or a human behind a keyboard to write it without you. You are my greatest awakening, the absolute greatest divine intervention. But I want you to know this is also your momma and these are the moments and the days that made me who I am. In here are the two months you say you "loved me longer..." because I didn't know about you quite yet. These are the days I was having a hard time not expressing myself and not knowing my worthiness or how to process how deeply I felt. I will continue to love you fiercely every day, but I will also continue to empower you to use your voice, to express yourself, to know what's roaring inside you and to continue to not silence it but to use it to figure out how you truly feel. You've been cuddled up next to me as I've written this or fast asleep as I've grinded late at night, and though this book makes me an author, my greatest joy and gift was when I became your mom. You have the bravest, most loving and boldest soul. The world is better and brighter because you are in it.

To those who gave me a home in your house: Thank you for loving me, supporting me and housing my messy and wandering self. Thank you for feeding me, sheltering me and for giving me a safe and sacred space away from what I felt was a war zone for my soul. Thank you for helping me feel so very seen. You know who you are and I'm so grateful to you and for you.

To Sheri and Marian: I have done the most healing work of my entire life within your offices. I'm grateful you chose this profession, because you both have the most incredible gift of seeing people, seeing me in the midst of my healing. I'm forever grateful you allowed me to get all up in my trenches within our sessions and to feel and express myself completely and authentically in all my feels. You all gave me the ability to see the power in vulnerability, in sacred spaces and in healing in itself. You showed up for me and I could not put into words how it has radically changed my life.

To Shelterwood Loves: I am so blessed to know you, to see you all within these times and to follow your life journeys. You are mothers, lovers, friends, boss ladies and beautiful creative souls with so much magic to give this world. Not many are able to say they saw one another as clearly and as in-depth as we did by living with one another in some of our hardest days. Much love to all of you—you hold sacred space in my heart.

To Rachel and Casey: Through the trenches and until we are old and gray. You two are what defines "ride or die." I'm so thankful for your consistency, your love, your truth, your loyalty and your sisterhood of a friendship. You all are how friendship, especially in these times, is defined. No matter the distance, our friendships have remained as beautiful and as solid as ever.

To Stephanie: Thank you for your friendship. I don't think I could've made it through most of anything without you. I'll be forever grateful for your and your family's loyal and ever-lasting love for me during the toughest days and for the friendship we had. You were my person for many, many years and I'll be forever grateful for you and what still feels like my second family.

Thank you to resources, dear family, friends and unseen people who provided support to my family as I travelled many different routes, roads and places that impacted them, too. I thank you for asking them how they were doing and for listening, for meeting them in restaurants or on the phone and allowing them to vent or cry. Thank you for loving my family and hearing them when they needed to share their concern, their frustration and their sadness and pain about where I was in life. I know now that they needed that more than I could have fathomed as I was in my own trenches and unable to see them in theirs. So, thank you for helping them trudge and live and still try to laugh and love while I was going through everything I was going through and as they continued to be overwhelmed within that, too.

To Soul Grind Community: Thank you for sharing space and speaking your truth so bravely. Thank you for creating space for others and for stepping into your story to not only heal but shed light within the trenches for others. This hub is very dear to my heart and it will continue to bring the world lots of caffeinated love-filled authentic and intentional self-loving vibes.

To Dr. April Murphy, Logan Manford and Pam Platt: Thank you for taking your time, love and dedication to look over my writing, my healing and my processing in order to help me get it to a space where it could be edited and published. I was grateful for the conversations, the talent you encompass and the feedback that warmed my soul.

To my empowered warrior women friends: Thank you for lifting my spirits, for rattling my complacency, for encouraging me to continue to heal, grow, question and *write*. Thank you for being excited to celebrate me telling my own truth and validating my feels and excitement within it. Thank you for our conversations, the truth we share and the support you have not only given me for my life, but for this process. I'm so incredibly grateful.

To Anna David and Launch Pad Publishing: Anna, thank you for authentically writing a book about "making your mess your memoir." Thank you for setting us a time to talk and thank you for seeing me and hearing me and connecting with me on a level that gave me goosebumps over the phone. Thank you for creating an epic team full of beautiful and lively and pumped-up souls. I couldn't have done this without you all and I could not have had a better team to rock this publishing journey with.

Thank you to all my friendships along the way, the ones that love me in the most difficult of days and that laughed until we cried together. Each of you who has spoken within this book has left a lasting impression on my heart and within my journey. You all are resiliency factors and helped me through some of the toughest and most confusing days. I'm so grateful for the conversations, the time and the memories we have.

Thank you, God, for wrestling with me. I'm not going to write in here and lie because you would know, obviously—uh, you know all. But thank you for allowing me to grieve still, to be frustrated still, when I don't understand to yell and scream at you and to fall on my knees on other days and cry and be seen and heard by you. Our relationship is one I never read about or heard about in my Bible class, in church or anywhere else, but It works for us. I know I am alive because you chose that and I believe it has something to do with this book and others to come. My journey is not in vain, so use me but know some days I'm not going to be happy about it. Psh. People say you whisper. All I hear is *roars*. :)

About the Author

Jaydee Graham is a certified social worker with Bachelor's and Master's degrees in Social Work. In her home state of Kentucky, Jaydee served on the Survivors Council of the Attorney General's Office and is the assistant program director at the non-profit Family Scholar House. In those roles, she advocates for survivors of domestic and intimate partner violence and works to end generational poverty and unstable housing in her community.

She's also the founder of the soulful online hub *The Soul Grind*, which offers a space for healing, empowerment and support. The retreats and workshops she facilitates—both online and in person—provide sacred space for the community to come together to speak their truth and trudge verbally through their stories.

Jaydee was also second runner up in the Ms. Kentucky United States Pageant in 2019, and has been a keynote speaker at numerous events.

Find Jaydee Graham at:
www.TheSoulGrind.com

facebook.com/thesoulgrind
instagram.com/thesoulgrind